A Wo

Suzanne Wrack is the *Guardian* and *Observer* women's football correspondent; the first person to hold this role at a national newspaper. Her work has also been published in *FourFourTwo*, and she is a regular contributor to the *Guardian's Football Weekly* podcast. A member of Women in Football, Women in Journalism, the Sports Journalist Association and the Football Writers Association, Suzanne was highly commended in the Media Initiative of the Year category at the 2018 Women's Sport Trust 'Be A Game Changer' awards and was shortlisted for the Football Supporters Federation Writer of the Year.

A Woman's Game

The Rise, Fall, and Rise Again of Women's Football

SUZANNE WRACK

First published by Guardian Faber in 2022
Guardian Faber is an imprint of Faber & Faber Ltd,
Bloomsbury House, 74–77 Great Russell Street,
London WC1B 3DA

Guardian is a registered trade mark of
Guardian News & Media Ltd,
Kings Place, 90 York Way, London N1 9GU

Typeset by Typo•glyphix, Burton-on-Trent, DE14 3HE

Printed and bound by CPI Group (UK) Ltd, Croydon, CR0 4YY

A CIP record for this book
is available from the British Library

ISBN 978–1–78335–215–9

FSC
www.fsc.org
MIX
Paper | Supporting
responsible forestry
FSC® C171272

2 4 6 8 10 9 7 5 3

Contents

Introduction   1

PART ONE: The Rise and Fall

1 In the beginning   13
2 The first official match   22
3 Dick, Kerr Ladies   34
4 Charity   45
5 The ban   55
6 Fifty years in the wilderness   67

PART TWO: From the Ashes

7 Lifted   79
8 Finding a way to play   88
9 The game goes official   98
10 The pioneers   113
11 Changing with the times   128
12 Streets of Oranje   143
13 Game-changing tournaments   150

PART THREE: Changing the Game

14 Professionalism   169
15 The tinkerman   181
16 The best   191
17 The elephant in the room   201

Conclusion: A manifesto   217
Acknowledgements   231
Photo credits   235
Index   237

Introduction

When you look at what football actually is, in its rawest form, it is initially hard to see how it has been able to become such a politically and financially powerful tool. It is, after all, only a sport that, like rugby, cricket and tennis, can be picked up by just about anyone. Yet football stands alone today as arguably commanding more respect and wielding greater power among ordinary people than many governments.

One hundred and fifty years since the laws of association football were first put down in a form that would still be familiar, at least in passing, to most of us, the game has changed enormously. And yet football retains this universality. Yes, clubs have become increasingly removed from the communities that birthed and sustained them, but still fans pour into grounds, hunch over TV screens, and consume content online like never before. And from the Syrian refugees using breeze blocks as goalposts to the glistening multi-million-pound academies of the world's top clubs, the game still remains, at heart, the same.

Throughout history, the accessibility and universal appeal of football have made it a powerful tool for fighting back against all forms of oppression, from Didier Drogba and his Ivory Coast teammates calling for an end to the civil war back home to Bundesliga clubs joining together against anti-immigration rhetoric, and from players taking a knee against racism to Marcus Rashford challenging the UK government over child food poverty.

It is this side of the game that I love reading about, writing about and exploring: how football can be used as a force for good. As a girl growing up in East London in the early 1990s, I could feel the power of the game on every warm day when, with the balcony windows of my family's council flat open, you could determine the score of the day's Arsenal men's match from the cheers that would emanate from the sofas around the estate. A community would be united in celebration, all the ways in which society divides us briefly overlooked.

Later, it would be in those fleeting moments of match-day euphoria that the self-consciousness I felt in being a woman at a football match would fade into the background. That fade was always brief. A look, a comment, being forced to brush past a tightly packed row of men to get to my seat, or a sexist chant that I would pretend to join in with – all would quickly remind me that I was different. It is perhaps unsurprising then that women's football is where I have found a home.

Women are simply one section of society – albeit one encompassing half of the global population – that has used football, and sport generally, to fight for influence and a more equitable society. Most female players would not say that this campaigning drive is what motivates them to play, or at least isn't why they started playing football. It is not a conscious thing; they are playing football because they enjoy it. But the mere act of playing football is unequivocally a feminist one.

Picking up a ball and heading to a patch of grass violates everything society expects of women – how they should look, how they should behave, how they should exercise, what they should wear and, at its core, how they should feel. For too long women have been made to feel like they don't belong in sport. I have seen this repeatedly over the years as I have explored the journeys of players from grassroots to elite, as well as in my own relationship with football.

Growing up, I wanted to be like my dad, wanted to like what he thought was cool. Fortunately, I was blessed with a father who was progressive and embraced and cultivated my love of football. However, he was the exception. In primary school I was the only girl that played football with the boys, the outlier who was shunted into goal, where no one else wanted to play. I wore boys' football shirts because girls' sizes and cuts did not exist. As I grew and my body changed, the shirts didn't quite fit; they were tighter around the top of the hips and there was no room for a developing bust. It increasingly felt like I was expected to grow out of sport.

My secondary school in Hackney was single-sex, with no boys for me to play against. I felt like I didn't fit in, but I tried to. PE, which seemed to avoid team sports, was universally hated and so I hated it too. For someone who spent the first eleven years of my life refusing dresses and skirts, suddenly I had to pull on a short, pleated skirt and over-sized pants to take part. I hated my body, a body that was stopping me from being welcomed in an arena I was so desperate to be a part of. I was self-conscious, I hated changing in front of my peers and I hated my period too. The more I avoided PE and the more I was driven from sport, the more

3

unfit I became and the less welcome I felt.

There were brief moments when I dipped back in. A handful of Arsenal Ladies players came and ran sessions after school for a couple of terms. I held the keepie-uppie record and revelled in those brief evenings dancing across the sports hall with a ball at my feet, but the damage had been done. Friends were bemused that I would stick behind after school, I had to walk home alone in the fading light, I felt unfit and the sessions were fleeting. I stopped. I became a spectator, in the stands where I didn't fit in either. How dare I, a young woman, encroach on this overwhelmingly male 'safe space'?

Times are changing. We live in a wildly different society to the one which existed at the time of the first forays of women into football, a very different society from twenty years ago when I was fourteen and grappling with the emotions discussed above, even. Women can vote, can divorce, can own property, can work, can be single. Yet even today, women's football provokes a vitriolic, misogynist defence of this space that many still consider the preserve of men. Why? Because despite the huge strides forward made by women, ingrained prejudices and oppressive views of a woman's place in society are still very much present. That is seen in boardrooms, in pay packets, in advertising, in the need to prevent women from having the right to choose what grows in their bodies, and far, far more.

And for some reason, the very idea of a woman pushing back against the system holding her down by entering a place of escapism 'for men' has always been a step too far for some. The first recorded official women's football match took place on 9 May 1881 between Scotland and England at Easter Road in Edinburgh, and the disdain from the press and public was palpable. Contempt for clothing, the standard of play and appearance dominated. Oh, how times have changed. Yet goalkeeper Helen Matthews (also known as Mrs Graham) persevered, and the game she organised saw the host nation finish victorious with a 3–0 win. Five days later, in front of 5,000 fans, a second game was abandoned after hundreds of men mobbed the pitch, forcing the players to flee on a horse-drawn bus.

Through more than a century of setbacks, bans and prejudices since, the resilient women's game has climbed off its knees time and time again. It has been fought for by women who could have easily given up or swapped into a sport more palatable to wider society. It has been driven both by those that desire change on a political and societal level but also by those who just enjoy the freedom of playing the game. Now, finally, women's football is seeing the investment and support it has been so lacking for so long. And yet, despite the ideological battles for women's right to play being won, it still gets attacked like no other sport. The trolls come out in force:

'It's rubbish.'
'The goalkeeping is terrible.'
'It's not fast enough.'
'Men's teams would beat them.'
'Women's football gets too much press coverage.'
'It's being shoved down our throats.'
'Non-league gets better crowds, but they don't get as much press.'

Yes, these are the voices of a minority, but it's a vocal one. And it's not new. In 1895, the *Daily Sketch* wrote scathingly of a British Ladies game: 'The first few minutes were sufficient to show that football by women, if the British Ladies be taken as a criterion, is totally out of the question. A footballer requires speed, judgement, skill, and pluck. Not one of these four qualities was apparent on Saturday. For the most part, the ladies wandered aimlessly over the field at an ungraceful jog-trot.'

Such close-minded attitudes are still all too pervasive today, more than a century later. The fight hasn't stopped. It may not be the same fight faced by the women of Nettie Honeyball's era, but football doesn't exist in a bubble. The prevailing attitudes in football necessarily reflect those in wider society. In a world where women still have to battle for reproductive rights, equal pay, maternity rights, childcare, education, or even the right to drive in some countries, so too have they had to continue to fight for the right to play professional sport, and all that entails, and in some cases any sport at all.

The US women's national team has in recent years taken to the courts to force a reluctant federation's hand and fight for equal pay and funding to match a men's team they outstrip both on the pitch and in revenue generated – a case that shatters the myth that equality comes naturally with growth, instead highlighting just how ingrained attitudes relating to the oppression of women are in society. They are not the only ones. Denmark, Colombia, Brazil, Scotland, the Republic of Ireland, Argentina and Norway are just some of the countries where female players have gone public in their fight for a bigger piece of the pie.

That Ada Hegerberg, the world's first female Ballon d'Or winner, was asked if she could twerk on stage following her 2018 victory shows that with every two steps forward there is a step back. Her decision to hang up her national team jersey aged just twenty-two, in protest at the direction of the domestic game in Norway and limited opportunities for young girls, shows there are many battles still to win.

Women's football is improving with every new aspect of professionalism. It is catching up. And to anyone who questions the level of the game we must ask a question. Would any of the men playing professionally today be as technically gifted, as physically fit or as mentally prepared if they had had to wash kits like Arsenal legend Alex Scott; fight fires full time like England goalkeeper Nicola Hobbs; go back to a homeless shelter after training like Reading's Fara Williams; cope with little to no medical or physio assistance for much of their careers; essentially have to pay to play; or complete six-hour round-trips after work to attend training?

This new generation of women footballers in countries where professionalism is slowly becoming a reality are starting to be relieved of those burdens. They are being set free, able to explore the uppermost limits of what they can achieve on a rectangle of grass. There is still a long way to go but we are welcoming in the most talented generation – and it's only going to get better. I, for one, am both desperately jealous of the opportunity afforded to today's young women and hugely relieved and buoyed by the fact that little girls today are welcome in football, with places to play, kit to wear, boots that fit.

This is a hugely exciting time. Clubs and federations need to sell it as such to boost the lowly domestic attendances that underpin the criticism. The record club attendances set in 2019, in Mexico, Spain, England and Italy, show that where there is a will there is a way. Clubs are investing. Their motivation to do so may not have been entirely philanthropic, nor solely driven by the fight for equality in a more gender-gap-conscious society, but how they have stumbled upon the potential of the women's game doesn't really matter. What does matter is that they recognise the quality of the players and the game, and show off their investment. Clubs and federations need to show their fans what they are producing, what they are investing in, and really sell it to them. Not with a few flash posters, or inspirational videos on social media. We don't need marketing – we need activism. Put the product in people's faces, in the places where they already absorb the game, and make them fall in love. Otherwise, what's the point?

Football is often called 'the beautiful game', but it is a 'beautiful game' that is increasingly removed from the realities of ordinary people. Ticket prices, jaw-dropping wage demands, more and more tenuous sponsorship deals, the cost of food and drink in grounds, corruption and mismanagement in the game's governing bodies: all these things are serving to isolate the very fans and communities that built the game. There is a drive to make the women's game a mirror of the men's, but do we really want it to be? We have the opportunity for it to be something better. In *A Woman's Game* we will chart the rise, fall, and rise again of women's football, following the circuitous path taken to its current heights, its relationship to the fight against oppression, what we want from it, what it can inspire and how we can get it there. This is a history of the game, as played by women, yes. But it is also, at heart, a manifesto for a better game.

ONE

The Rise and Fall

1 – In the beginning

On 10 May 1873 the satirical British magazine *Punch* mockingly warned that women's involvement in cricket would only lead one way. 'Irrepressible woman is again in the field,' it exclaimed. '"Ladies' Cricket" is advertised, to be followed, there is every reason to apprehend, by Ladies Fives, Ladies Football, Ladies Golf etc. It is all over with men. They had better make up their minds to rest contented with croquet, and afternoon tea, and sewing machines, and perhaps an occasional game at drawing-room billiards.'

The jesters weren't wrong. The first women's association football match was played just eight years after these words were written. And in fact, while match reports in the traditional sense only began to appear in the late nineteenth century, there are hints of women's involvement in football significantly earlier.

One of the earliest such mentions in British records occurs in 'A Dialogue Between Two Shepherds' by the poet and scholar Sir Philip Sidney (1554–86), in which one character says to the other:

> *A tyme there is for all, my mother often sayes,*
> *When she, with skirts tuckt very hy, with girles at football playes.*

There are also a number of accounts from eighteenth-century Scotland that tell of annual matches played between

13

single and married women, with an audience of bachelors casting their eyes over the footballing skills of potential partners. The Rev. Dr Alexander Carlisle wrote of one such fixture in the village of Inveresk in East Lothian in 1795: 'As [the fishwives] do the work of men, their manners are masculine and their strength and activity is equal to their work. Their amusements are more of the masculine kind. On holidays they frequently play golf; and on Shrove Tuesday there is a standing match at football between the married and unmarried women, at which the former are always victors.'

Putting aside the reality-TV-style sexual politics, what is interesting about this decidedly working-class form of matchmaking is that the most desirable attributes weren't looks or femininity, but rather a woman's physical strength and sporting prowess. In many ways this feels a thoroughly modern attitude, bringing to mind the 'This Girl Can' era of sports promotion, with muscles bulging, sweat dripping, make-up removed or smeared and all types of bodies welcomed. But here is an example from over two centuries ago demonstrating that frailty, paleness and slightness have not always existed as desirable features of women. Those views are man-made, products of various societies over the years that have devalued the role of women and placed men at the head of the metaphorical table.

Beyond Britain's shores can be found even earlier examples of women's involvement in sports closely related to the modern game. In China a game called *cuju*, or 'kickball', was played as far back as the Han dynasty, which ran from 206 BC to AD 220. Some aspects of *cuju* would be recognisable to the modern spectator: teams wore different coloured kits and competed to kick a ball into a net. Rather than today's armbands, however, captains wore hats with straight wings, differentiating them from the curling wings worn by other players. The game was popular among women, as indicated by a poem from the ninth century AD lauding the *cuju* performance of General Li Guangyan:

> *Quick as a monkey on the ballfield, with a falcon's grace*
> *Three thousand ladies tilted their heads to watch him*
> *Trampling shiny earrings as they crowded for a view*
> *Standards bobbed and waved, banners flashed and shone.*

And women were not merely spectators to *cuju* matches: paintings from the Han dynasty depict women with hair up, long sleeves and flowing dresses kicking and flicking balls in gardens. Again, any suggestion of the impropriety of women kicking a ball and daring to take an interest in the universally accessible sport is demonstrably a more modern invention.

Fast-forward to 9 May 1881 and we have the first formal reporting from a women's football match, in a game widely considered to have been the first recorded women's international. The *Glasgow Herald* described the match, which took place at Easter Road in Edinburgh, simply as 'rather novel':

> *A considerable amount of curiosity was evinced in the event, and upwards of a thousand persons witnessed it. The young ladies' ages appeared to range from eighteen to four-and-twenty, and they were very smartly dressed. The Scotch team wore blue*

jerseys, white knickerbockers, red stockings, a red belt, high-heeled boots and blue and white cowl: while their English sisters were dressed in blue and white jerseys, blue stockings and belt, high-heeled boots, and red and white cowl. The game, judged from a player's point of view, was a failure, but some of the individual members of the teams showed that they had a fair idea of the game. During the first half the Scotch team, playing against the wind, scored a goal, and in the second half they added another two, making a total of three goals against their opponents' nothing. Misses St Clair and Cole scored the first two, and the third was due to Misses Stevenson and Wright.

The match report, which was far more balanced than you perhaps would have expected, also included what is seemingly the first teamsheet of the women's game. This artefact offers a helpful insight into the women involved in that historic first outing, including the three Hopewell sisters, early counterparts of today's foremost footballing siblings such as Rosie and Mollie Kmita, Phil and Gary Neville or Ada and Andrine Hegerberg:

	Scotland	England
Goalkeeper:	Ethel Hay	May Goodwin
Backs:	Bella Osborne Georgina Wright	Mabel Hopewell Maud Hopewell

Half-backs:	Rose Rayman	Maud Starling
	Isa Stevenson	Ada Everston
Forwards:	Emma Wright	Geraldine Vintner
	Louise Cole	Mabel Vance
	Lily St Clair	Eva Davenport
	Maud Riweford	Minnie Hopewell
	Carrie Balliol	Kate Mellon
	Minnie Brymner	Nelly Sherwood

This first match was the brainchild of Edinburgh-based theatre entrepreneur and actor Alec Gordon, who had watched the growing popularity of men's international football and saw an opportunity to capitalise on the interest by using women players. Working with Charles Scholes, the head of a theatrical empire, and Scholes's theatre manager, George Fredrick Charles, they drew players from dance and performing circles. The majority of the England side and several of the Scottish team were members of Lizzie Gilbert's Juvenile Ballet Company, while the remaining Scots were recruited from the Princess's Theatre house company. Gordon and Charles themselves appear in a later account of the match in the *Glasgow Herald* as 'umpires' managing Scotland and England respectively.

Today there is a clamouring for society to recognise the potential value of the women's game, both from an economic and social point of view. Slowly the momentum has swung behind the women's game as the men's game begins to top out, with the marketplace saturated when it comes to sponsorship opportunities and broadcasting slots. Yet here, in the late 1800s, you have the earliest records of individuals drawing conclusions on the potential of the women's game far ahead of schedule.

News of the game would spread across the country, filtering into local newspapers, and even gaining international attention with the *New York Sun*, *Sydney Evening News* and *Montreal Daily Mail* all carrying reports of the game.

Several reports mocked the quality of the game but it is frankly ludicrous for the women, playing in 'high-heeled boots' in their first advertised fixture, to be expected to be playing to the same standard as the men. The *Dunfermline Journal* noted that more than half of those in attendance, who were clearly unwilling to contextualise the fledgling sport before them, had left before the end; they also reported that the match was apparently played without controversy. The teams would go on to face a very different response in Glasgow the following week, on 16 May, however.

'What will probably be the first and last exhibition of a female football match in Glasgow took place on Monday evening on Shawfield Grounds,' reported the *Nottinghamshire Guardian* the following day.

Over 5,000 predominantly male fans had gathered at Shawfield for the second meeting of the English and Scottish ladies' sides, but it seemed that the novelty was already beginning to wear off. The *Nottinghamshire Guardian* reported that:

The meagre training of the teams did not augur much for proficiency of play and if the display of football tactics was of a sorry description, it was only what might have been expected, and not much worse than some of the early efforts of our noted football clubs. The costume was suitable, and at a distance the players could scarcely have been distinguished from those in ordinary football matches. The game was continued without interruption till ends were changed, but the chaff of the spectators was anything but complimentary.

At last a few roughs broke into the enclosure, and as these were followed by hundreds soon after, the players were roughly jostled, and had prematurely to take refuge in the omnibus which had conveyed them to the ground. Their troubles were not, however, yet ended, for the crowd tore up the stakes and threw them at the departing vehicle, and but for the presence of the police some bodily injury to the females might have occurred. The team of four grey horses was driven rapidly from the ground amid the jeers of the crowd, and the players escaped with, let us hope, nothing worse than a serious fright.

Subsequent matches between the two sides took place without incident in Blackburn and Bradford, before things again turned ugly at Cheetham Football Club's ground in Tetlow Fold on 20 June. The teams were half an hour late onto the pitch, and while the crowd was a paying one, the majority in attendance were reported as having 'managed to elude the vigilance of the gatekeepers'. Frustrated by the delayed start and 'after some indifferent play, which lasted something like half-an-hour, the ring was broken into and the wildest confusion prevailed, the players having to make good their escape'.

Under the headline 'Disorderly Scene at a Women's Football Match' the *Manchester Guardian* was critical of the proceedings:

The score or so of young women who do not hesitate to gratify vulgar curiosity by taking part in what is termed a 'ladies' football match appeared last evening for the second time this week, on the ground of Cheetham Football Club, Tetlow Fold, Great Cheetham street. The Club, however, had nothing to do with the affair. The public had been invited by placard to witness a match between 'eleven of England' and 'eleven of Scotland', the kick-off to take place at half-past seven pm. The players attired in a costume which is neither graceful nor very becoming, were driven to the ground in a wagonette, and, as was to be expected, were followed by a crowd largely composed of youths, rather to avail themselves of the opportunity presented for a little boisterous amusement.

Very few persons paid for admission to the grounds, but a great multitude assembled in the road and struggled for a sight of what was going on within the enclosure, whilst an equally large number gathered on the higher ground on the other side of the field for a similar purpose. A number of police constables were present to maintain order and prevent any one entering without paying, and for about an hour whilst the so-called match was being played they succeeded. There were frequent attempts, however, to elude the constables. At length a great rush was made by those occupying the higher land, and the football ground was speedily taken possession of by the mob. Apprehending a repetition of the rough treatment they have met with in other parts of the country the women no sooner heard

*the clamour which accompanied the rush than they also took
to their heels and ran to where their wagonette was standing.
This they reached before the crowd could overtake them, and
amid the jeers of the multitude and much disorder they were
immediately driven away.*

Seemingly unperturbed by the furore and boosted by
the healthy gate receipts, the teams still did not stop and
would go on to play two games in Liverpool towards the
end of June 1881 before the reports of their activity begin
to peter out. This was by no means the end of women's
football in the nineteenth century, but it wouldn't be until
1895 that the fixture that would eventually be recognised
by FIFA, the global governing body of football, as the first
official women's football match was played. These early
fixtures paved the way, though, and the players and team
organisers displayed a determination, a resilience and fore-
sight (in their belief of the potential of the women's game)
that is mirrored throughout the entire history of women's
football.

2 – The first official match

WANTED, several LADIES to play another Ladies' Team for
a FOOTBALL MATCH during November; share of gate-
money; opportunity for practice on private ground afforded.
— Write, Miss P., 27, Weston Park, Crouch End, N.

So read the advert placed in *The Graphic* in 1894 that
would eventually lead to the foundation of the British
Ladies' Football Club. The house of 'Miss P.' belonged
to the Smith family, of which Phoebe, one of the team's
early players, was the youngest. Her older brothers Alfred
Hewitt Smith and Frederick Smith were, according to various newspaper reports, also involved in running the club.

The name most frequently associated with the first official women's team is not that of the Smith family, however,
but that of Nettie Honeyball. Honeyball is widely believed
to be the pseudonym of a middle-class Londoner called
Mary Hutson, who also lived in Crouch End. She acted
as a figurehead for the club both as secretary and captain,
as well as describing herself in interviews as its founder.
Honeyball was also responsible for recruiting the aristocrat
and suffragette Lady Florence Dixie, who became president and financier of the team.

In 1894 the bestselling illustrated weekly magazine *The
Sketch*, picking up on the moves of women into the game,
produced a mocking cartoon. In it a huddle of high-class
women in dresses surround a fainting referee, while a

woman heading a ball is tackled rugby-style to the ground, alongside the caption 'Oh bother the rules'. Elsewhere men leer over 'the good looking goal-keeper', and women make the most of the half-time break to fan themselves and do each other's hair.

The elite mocked, but there was no stopping the momentum. Honeyball and the Smith family pulled together a group of thirty-plus women keen to be involved and in *The Sketch* itself, on 6 February, explained the motivations for doing so in an interview. 'Miss Nettie J. Honeyball is the secretary and captain of what may be fairly described as the sporting sensation of the hour, and, if energy and enthusiasm can command success, then surely is the association already preassured of victory,' the interview began.

As I saw her in her pretty little study in Crouch End, a thoughtful-looking young lady, with a strong personality, I at once dispelled the suspicion of burlesque that came into my mind. 'You are quite right,' said Miss Honeyball, putting aside an ominous batch of correspondence to give me some details; 'there is nothing of the farcical nature about the British Ladies' Football Club. I founded the association late last year, with the fixed resolve of proving to the world that women are not the "ornamental and useless" creatures men have pictured. I must confess, my convictions on all matters, where the sexes are so widely divided, are all on the side of emancipation, and I look forward to the time when ladies may sit in Parliament and have a voice in the direction of affairs, especially those which concern them most.'

What is clear, and utterly fascinating, is that the motivation for forming the team went far beyond just a love of the game – although that was, explicitly, the starting point. Honeyball makes clear that she saw the aims of the club much more broadly and believed it could be used as a tool to challenge the outdated views around women in society and further the emancipation of women. The involvement of the feminist Lady Dixie, author of the utopian novel *Gloriana, or the Revolution of 1900*, in which women win suffrage, would likely have been proffered on the basis of the political impact the club could have rather than its sporting impact.

Asked whether she anticipated a future in which clubs employed both male and female players, Honeyball replied: 'Such a consummation is, of course, very far distant, but it is possible. You must remember we do not profess to the strength of men . . . but we claim the science, and, in my opinion, football is just the exercise to promote health and grace among women.'

Honeyball could never have predicted that it would be over one hundred years before clubs having women's teams would be the norm or that in 2022 we would still be a world away from an equal game. Now, there are a host of brands, clubs, sponsors and players reaching towards and seeing the potential in the women's game that Honeyball, and those involved in the first match not long before, saw and desired more than a hundred years ago.

Honeyball was confident that her players had the mental fortitude to stand up to any hostility from spectators of the fledgling game, saying:

When Lady Florence Dixie consented to become president, she specially stipulated that, if the club were to attain its end, the girls should enter into the spirit of the game with heart and soul. 'I will have nothing to do with balloon-sleeves and trained skirts, and anything like that,' she said; 'don't court ridicule by ridiculing yourselves.' Accordingly, we all have our costumes of divided skirts – a sort of blue serge knickerbocker – and the teams will be distinguished by wearing, respectively, cardinal and pale-blue blouses. You will detect no nervousness in the girls when they make their first public appearance. We practise twice a week.

Lady Dixie and Honeyball had been involved in campaigns for gender-neutral clothing and in carrying those principles into their team they were again ahead of their time. Although there have always been fringe movements and campaigns that have attacked the way society has established and maintains gender roles through clothing, it is only in recent years that campaigns such as 'Let Toys be Toys' have begun to highlight how traditional gender roles are reinforced through children's clothing and toys. In the late 1800s these women were using football to advance gender equality.

Honeyball did not struggle to recruit members to the team, and – barring some 'bogus applications from young men' – the advert attracted close to thirty players varying from fifteen to twenty-six in age. They were overwhelmingly from across London but some travelled in from further afield.

'I called all the ladies to a meeting, and we soon proceeded to business,' said Honeyball.

*None of them, of course, had previously played, but, like myself,
had gained all their experience and love of football from frequent
onlooking. Then came the question of ground. The committee
of the Oval refused to allow us the use of that ground, and
eventually we made arrangements with Mr. C. W. de Lyons Pike
to practise and play on the Nightingale Lane enclosure. We have
been out so far very regularly, no matter what the weather, and
each time the improvement in style is more marked. Mr. J. W.
Julian, the well-known half-back [with Tottenham], is acting as
coach, and rendering valuable assistance.*

She added: 'Of course, when we first began, complaints were
made of stiffness and soreness, but that soon wore off, and you
would be surprised to see the energy thrown into the game.'

The *Sketch* interviewer concluded: 'Since interviewing
Miss Honeyball, I have had the pleasure of witnessing the
members of the B.L.F.C. at practice, and must confess to a
feeling of surprise at the amount of ability already attained.
Although the occasion of my visit was not favourable,
meteorologically, the ladies went about their various duties
pluckily and energetically, skill and shooting power making
up for any lack of speed and force.'

In this patronising close it is clear that many of the arguments against women's football that we hear in the twenty-first
century – 'it's rubbish/slow/not as good as the men's game'
– have been ever-present. Moreover, as is often the case
today, the journalism at the close of the nineteenth century
refrained from contextualising the fledgling sport of women's
football, instead pitting it against the more established men's
game from the off.

The context matters. Women were taking part for the first time and pushing against attitudes that said keeping fit was not for them. Nonetheless they were expected to put on as good a show as men who had been playing for a number of years, and for whom sports, fitness and competition were encouraged and embedded into their day-to-day lives.

Women had and have always worked. In feudal society, when agriculture was dominant, women and girls would work the fields and farms with their husbands, fathers and brothers. It was not work for a wage, which would have been completely unpalatable to men, but more acceptable feminine chores.

In the Victorian era, with the onset of industrialisation, working women became much more visible and more visibly separated from the home. As the factories sprang up, women went to work in them, with the textile mills and coal mines in particular drawing on women, a cheaper source of labour as they were paid less, to bolster the workforce. That created a clash between societal expectations of a woman's place in the world and the necessity of female workers in these new industrialised workplaces. The industrial and economic need was stronger. As a result a new, paid workforce of women was showing signs of independence from men.

'You've got people like the match women arm in arm, hundreds strong, singing songs, swearing, being cheeky, being disrespectful to passers-by. This is seen as awful,' says historian Dr Louise Raw, author of *Striking a Light*, which tells the story of the famous strike action by women match makers at the Bryant and May factory in 1888. 'It is not happening far away in the countryside anymore; it is on the

27

streets of towns and cities. There are big groups of women workers who become very important.'

Women were making strides, and the establishment wanted to put that genie back in the bottle. Whether the ruling classes liked it or not, however, women were proving themselves vital to the British economy. Another effect of industrialisation was that the most vulnerable in society suddenly became more visible – instead of starving in the fields, out of sight and out of mind, they were in the cities in unmissable numbers. So the establishment had two problems: women and inequality. Their response was depressingly predictable: 'It was the perfect solution, as it always has been throughout history. All the social problems that you can see – drunkenness, homelessness, neglected children – it is because Mum is at work for sixteen hours a day. Working women, it's all their fault,' says Raw.

As we have already discussed, women have always had to work. The concept of a 'breadwinner wage' (that one person in a household could earn enough to keep the whole family fed and looked after) was, and still is, a myth for the overwhelming majority of society. Employers will not suddenly, magically, become very generous and start paying men enough for the whole family because, well, why would they?

But it is this myth – that everyone will be able to survive happily on the man's wage and that that will allow woman back in her natural role at home – that was used to place the blame on working women for society's ills. If women were in the home then the men would come home for dinner rather than going to the pub, eliminating drunkenness and calming down the rowdy working class. If men had a stable home life there would be no need for prostitution. If women were looking after the kids full time then the issue of child mortality (around half of children in poverty in the late nineteenth century died before their fifth birthday) would be solved. So just as modern women's football begins, working-class women are being absolutely demonised left, right and centre.

What did it mean to be a lady at that time? 'It's an absence of noise, of dirt, of movement, of sex, of drinking, of laughing. It is sitting very, very quietly, very, very still. It's as far away from the messiness of being human as you can get, it's horribly repressive and it's physically restrictive – with the clothing and with the corsets and with the crinolines,' says Raw.

'So a woman footballer? That's terrifying. It's just about okay if a middle-class lady is doing lawn tennis or a bit of croquet because you can wear your long skirt for that, and take in some jolly good exercise so you can rear nice healthy children for the Empire, that's important.'

This is why Honeyball, Lady Dixie and others were keen to portray the women players of the late 1800s as having been drawn from the upper middle classes. While the reality was that many of the women involved came from the lower-class world of theatre and dance groups, a façade of upper-class acceptability was key to the effectiveness of their rebellion.

In the eyes of the establishment, working-class women were rough, immoral and neglectful. The mere idea of them playing football would have been considered unbelievably horrifying. Portraying the most prominent women's footballers as middle class and married sidestepped those criticisms: these

29

were proper, respectable women that had to be taken more seriously.

This, as with so many aspects of their campaign, was a calculated sleight of hand on the part of the suffragettes. With a nation so in love with football, from the upper classes in their school playing fields to the workers in their factory teams, it was only natural that the attentions of the women's rights movement would be drawn towards the game. What better way to get right to the heart of the masculine world than with football?

Such an attention-grabbing tactic was not without its risks, however. The suffragettes faced horrific levels of opposition, including violence and sexual assault from the police and the groups of anti-suffrage men who would go out and attack women on suffragette processions.

'There's a big risk for these women,' says Raw. 'When the early football match in Glasgow is driven off the pitch it's an echo of what happens later to suffragettes. The Victorian era is seen as a chivalrous time but my God if you step out of line, whether it's campaigning for the vote or playing football, you soon see that men are entirely prepared to take you out of the category of lady and put you in the category of women – and you could give a good slap to a woman or you could sexually abuse a woman. If you stepped out of line the privileges of your sex got revoked pretty quickly.'

For the inaugural match of the British Ladies' Football Club, over 10,000 would turn up to watch. 'We hope it will be their last,' declared the London *Evening Standard* editorial two days later on 25 March 1895. 'To say football was played would be stating more than the real truth,' opined the paper's match report. 'The whole affair was a huge farce,' said *The Sketch*'s full-page report of the sixty-minute match in which the 'North' team defeated the 'South' team 7–1. The *Evening Standard* continued:

Some of these young persons appeared to possess only an elementary knowledge of the game and its laws, and, for the present at all events, the Club is quite unlikely to attract spectators for the sake of the play. How long it will continue to attract them for reasons unconnected with sport is another matter; but it is significant that a considerable proportion of those present on Saturday left the field at half-time. The laughter was easy and the amusement rather coarse; but these are waning delights, and we shall be surprised if a second display wins even so equivocal a success as the first. The probability is, we trust, that in a very short time the Club will die a natural and unlamented death.

Neither by training, nor for the most part by constitution, are women adapted for games like football, which are necessarily rough. It is pleasant to find them devoting themselves to active exercises of a suitable kind, which add to their physical charms without in any degree diminishing the greatest of all their attractions – modesty; but it cannot be pretended that football is either a decent or an elegant occupation for girls, and we can only regard the new Club as a passing whim, an ephemeral vulgarity. The fancy shirts and blue knicker-bockers may look very smart and daring when the rival teams are photographed in repose, but they are not set off to advantage when the figures are in motion. If the lady football player wishes to be taken seriously as a sports-woman, she must be told plainly that she is not a success.

31

By all means, let women have suitable opportunities for recreation and physical exercise, which are as necessary to them as to men; but their own good sense will be sufficient to convince them that football is one of the sports in which they look ridiculous when they fail, and would only become un-feminine if they were by any chance to succeed. A lady in a scrimmage – the thing is unthinkable.

Again, the fledgling women's game is being compared to the men's game as opposed to the latter being viewed as a benchmark for the new sport. Interestingly, the suitability of the game for women is being questioned with greater and greater vigour, while the perennial male gaze is explicit in the statement that football is not a good way for women to show off their bodies compared to other forms of exercise that help provide necessary fitness without impacting on modesty or diminishing the 'physical charms' of women.

As with the team of 1881, the predictions of a quick death of the BLFC were premature. The team began to tour and in four months played up and down the country, from Ashton Gate in Bristol to Gigg Lane in Bury, and from Springvale Park in Glasgow to Falcon Cliff on the Isle of Man, with thousands in attendance.

By the start of the following season in 1896 the press interest was waning and the team had seemingly split, with goalkeeper Mrs Graham confirming to the *Hull Daily Mail* that a rival team had been set up and Lady Dixie's patronage was gone (she had pulled her support as a result of her name being used by both teams). But women continued to play up and down the country, sometimes with men helping make up the numbers. There is mention of the British Ladies' Football Club even as late as 1905, with an article in the *Norfolk Chronicle* headlined 'Lady Footballers for Norwich' announcing a charity match to be played between the women's team and an XI of the 'stronger sex'.

However, the early 1900s would prove to be a more barren period for women's football, with organised matches by and large being replaced by ad hoc ladies' games at fairs and garden parties, with many matches played against men. 'A successful and highly amusing football match took place at Blackpool yesterday afternoon, between teams representing "Ladies" and "Gentlemen",' wrote the *Hartlepool Northern Daily Mail* of one such game on 11 January 1906. 'The "Ladies" were members of the sterner sex, gorgeously attired in all kinds of extravagant costumes, and equally comical and grotesque were the "Gentlemen". The comic element prevailed throughout the match, although a fair amount of regard was paid to the rules of the game, and the referee, who significantly affected the uniform of police sergeant, was most gallant towards the "Ladies". The fair ones eventually won by three goals to one.'

There was more to this dry period, where there seems to be a fairly definitive end to formal matches and a step back to the game being played for entertainment rather than sport, than meets the eye – and we'll revisit that later on. However, despite the sport's retreat in the early 1900s women's football would soon experience a seismic revival that would have an impact far beyond the pitch and would rattle both the footballing and non-footballing establishment.

3 – Dick, Kerr Ladies

After more than a decade of informality and obscurity for women's football the First World War changed the narrative. No one could have predicted the seismic effect it would have on women at its outbreak in 1914.

As we have seen, women already formed a significant part of the industrial workforce by the early 1900s, albeit mainly concentrated in textiles. The war would lead to an even more dramatic increase in the volume of women workers in industrial workplaces, however, particularly in the more manual jobs previously deemed unsuitable. All this would have an immeasurable impact not only on women themselves but also on the way society generally viewed them.

The introduction of conscription in 1916 accelerated this workplace revolution even further, with munitions factories becoming the largest employer of women by 1918. Early resistance to women moving into industry, particularly these more manual roles, crumbled as all fit men between the ages of eighteen and forty-one were thrust into the battles being waged on the continent. Gaps were left in workplaces up and down the country and women stepped in, with the government coordinating recruitment drives.

The same was true internationally. In Germany, by 1917, nearly 1.4 million women were a part of the wartime workforce. Ammunitions factory Krupp employed next to no women in 1914 but three years later some 30 per cent of its employees were female. Before the US entered the fray in April 1917 thousands of American women joined and set up volunteer groups and charities dedicated to providing support and relief to the victims in war-torn Europe, and American nurses served in England, Serbia, Russia, France and Germany. Once the country had formally declared its involvement, American women began to fill the roles of men headed for the front and, despite resistance, for the first time women served in the Army and Navy as nurses and telephone operators.

Factories weren't the only traditionally male workplaces where women made up the gaps. In England they became railway guards, ticket collectors, postal workers, formed Women's Patrols as part of the police, and became bus conductors and drivers, bank tellers, civil servants and farm-hands. This wasn't a gradual, natural shift in the outlook of society, but a sudden and total paradigm change. In a short space of time working women had gone from being encouraged to stay home to being told by the government and ruling classes to fill out the depleted workforces to maintain the war effort.

All women were drawn into the fold, making it harder for working women to be blamed for all society's ills. However, the class divide was still very much alive. While working-class women primarily filed onto the production lines, middle- and upper-class women keen to do their bit volunteered, did police work, fundraised for injured soldiers, went into nursing and became supervisors. A small number formed voluntary units and travelled to mainland Europe to drive ambulances, provide first aid and run soup kitchens closer to the action. The middle and upper classes were motivated by patriotism and pushed by the relentless propaganda, but the war also offered them stimulation and excitement far beyond what they had been afforded prior.

The result of all this was that women were now a part of Britain's workforce on a scale not seen before. This sudden upswell built a camaraderie and collectivism that also saw women became organised in trade unions. Despite coming into jobs vacated by men, they were still not paid the same or afforded the same rights and conditions. The war might have paused certain elements of the suffrage campaign but patriotism and propaganda were not enough to quell the fight for equal pay. In 1918, with the war still raging, women working on London's buses and trams took strike action demanding the same war bonuses as the men. It was the first equal pay strike in Britain, likely inspired by movements such as the 1909 strike of 20,000 textile workers in New York and the 1917 International Women's Day strikes of women textile workers in St Petersburg that would trigger the shutdown of most factories in the city, as well as the start of the Russian Revolution itself.

It was against this backdrop that women's football had its resurgence. Morale was important on the front lines, but it was also seen as being crucial back home in Britain. The contribution of everyone to the war effort was critical and the government and bosses had to attempt to keep this new workforce motivated, happy and productive. So they could overlook this newly empowered mass of women taking up a pastime they had previously deemed inappropriate. In addition, one of the biggest arguments against women playing was, at that time, moot. Women were working in the same dangerous and physically demanding positions that men had previously occupied, so any attempt to prevent women playing football on the basis of physical suitability was laughable.

Where the ruling classes had organised football and codified it, with versions played in private schools such as Eton, Harrow and Winchester, it was in the factories and pubs and among the working classes that it would find its mass appeal and begin to turn into the game we know today. By the First World War the men's game was developed, had a professional league and was a popular spectator sport. Industrialisation gave workers fixed hours, and thus free time, and shifted the working masses into the city and away from the physically demanding roles of the countryside. In doing so it also helped football become a popular hobby, both for fitness and as a way to spend free time.

The war saw working women find sport in the same way, during their own period of mass industrialisation, and bosses and the establishment encouraged it. They began to play football during their lunch breaks, which led to teams being formed up and down the country. The munitions factories in particular, where the work was most dangerous, became a focal point for the development of the women's game.

The British newspaper archives reveal quite how quickly this change in uptake of women's football came about. Between 1913 and 1915 there are on average only eight mentions a year of the game. By 1916 this increases to twenty-three mentions, followed by 318 the following year and 276 in 1918.

One example is the *Sheffield Daily Telegraph*'s report from 27 December 1916 of a match played by the city's munitions factory workers. Under the tagline 'Funny football' it reads:

Truly the great war has, indeed, brought about abundant changes in the customs of both men and women, and if, say less than three years ago, one even suggested that a ladies' football match would attract a 'gate' of nearly 10,000 people, the idea would have been treated as a huge joke. However, time works changes, and we have had many illustrations where the fair sex have invaded almost every industry which, before the war, was left to 'mere man'. Now they have taken to football.

At the Vickers' Sports ground, Carbrook, yesterday morning, a match was played between the lady munition workers employed at Messrs. Vickers, Ltd. The opposing teams were the East Projectile Shop versus the South (1 and 2) Shops. Long before the match was timed to start huge crowds made the journey by foot and tram, and when it was time to kick-off the attendance bordered close upon 10,000. The organiser of the match, Mr. Alfred Preston, has done his work exceptionally well. He has had the ready help of Messrs. C. and S. Smith, and the munition girls of Sheffield have during the past few weeks been exceptionally busy in the direction of selling tickets. As a result of the effort it is expected that a sum upwards of £100 will be handed over to the Wounded Soldiers' Fund. Immediately the girls entered the playing piece they received a rousing cheer from the large assemblage. The South team appeared in red, whilst the East sported Aston Villa's colours. Mrs. J. W. Robinson kicked off, and very quickly the fun commenced. To attempt to describe the game would be superfluous, but at halftime neither side had scored. The second half showed indications that the players had had enough. Finally the doom of the East side was sealed when Miss Nellie Marshall placed the leather well past the custodian's reach, and this, of course, brought further vociferous cheering from the crowd. South kept the lead until the whistle blew, and the result was: South 1, East 0.

Mr. Alfred Preston 'officiated' as referee, and had very little difficulty in detecting any fouls, whilst Messrs. C. and S. Smith had quite a busy time running the lines. There were about 70 wounded soldiers present, and they, along with the other spectators, thoroughly enjoyed the fun.

The tone of this report is markedly different to the much more critical eye cast in the late 1800s and that is perhaps reflective of the broader shift in attitudes forced by the necessities of war. Throughout the war women played and, with the men's professional game halted, both sexes would go to watch.

The most famous factory team was born in the Dick, Kerr factory in Preston. Originally a railway and tram plant, it was converted into a munitions factory during the war and was also drafted into the production of aircraft and loco-motives. By 1917 the converted factory was churning out a staggering 30,000 shells per week.

No one was untouched by tragedy during that period. Many of the women and girls working in munitions fac-tories during the war had lost brothers, fathers and husbands themselves. The need to maintain morale could not have been greater, and in factories across the country football be-came a tool for keeping spirits and productivity up. At Dick,

Kerr the women began playing football with the men at the factory during the tea breaks and lunchtimes.

'The lads had had a bad run of results. The girls were giving them some stick one particular day and Grace Sibbet said something like: "you call yourself a football team, we could do better than you lot", because they had been beaten again. The men were a bit miffed, their pride was hurt, so they challenged the girls to play them in a proper match,' explains Gail Newsham, Dick, Kerr Ladies historian and author of *In a League of Their Own*, which charts the team's story.

'Grace was the inspiration behind it and she got the girls together. They played in this match, of which nobody knows the result – I'd like to think that they won but I don't know,' Newsham laughs.

After this first game, the matron of the local military hospital where injured soldiers were being treated approached the Dick, Kerr factory to ask if the female workers would help to raise some money for the soldiers over Christmas. She had suggested a charity concert but the women thought it would be a good idea to have a charity match instead. That offering would spark to life one of the most important teams in the history of women's football.

Sadly, Grace Sibbet would not be able to continue playing for the team she had spearheaded, as she was struck down with tuberculosis, but some of the players in that first practice match also went on to play in the subsequent charity game, which was held on Christmas Day 1917 at Deepdale, the main stadium of the Preston North End men's team (a badge of honour still rarely afforded to women's teams today).

Alfred Frankland worked in the offices of the factory and was a member of the company's sports committee. Watching from his office window as the women played in their lunch breaks, he sensed an opportunity. Known as an efficient organiser with a flair for marketing, he would take on the team and end up devoting much of the rest of his life to its development.

A staggering 10,000 people would watch the Christmas Day charity game, which raised £600 (equivalent to just under £43,000 in 2020) for injured soldiers. The *Lancashire Evening Post*'s Boxing Day match report was very favourable, no doubt in part because of the effect the war had had on the wider perception of the worth of working, active women, and the fact that this was a novel way to help the poor wounded men:

There were 10,000 people at Deepdale yesterday afternoon at the ladies' football match between teams representing the munition workers of Dick, Kerr's and Coulthard's, and the appearance of the historic enclosure was quite like old times. The proceeds from the sale of tickets, which were supplemented by a collection taken by wounded soldiers on the ground, were for Moor Park Hospital, and when all the money has been got in the funds the institution should receive a handsome windfall. The players, who were understood to have been in strict training for the encounter, wore orthodox football costume, jerseys, dark blue shorts, and regulation boots. Coulthard's were in red and white stripes and Dick, Kerr's in black and white, with the addition of natty, close-fitting hats to match. Corsets were barred. So far as appearances went, Dick, Kerr's seemed to hold some advantage between two athletic-looking sides. Miss Hollins kicked off.

After the Christmas dinner the crowd were in the right humour for enjoying this distinctly war-time novelty. There was a tendency amongst the players at the start to giggle, but they soon settled down to the game in earnest. Dick, Kerr's were not long in showing that they suffered less than their opponents from stage fright, and had a better all-round idea of the game. Woman for woman they were also speedier, and had a larger share of that quality which in football slang is known as 'heftiness'. Quite a number of their shots at goal would not have disgraced the regular professional except in direction, and even professionals have been known on occasion to be a trifle wide of the target. Their forward work, indeed, was often surprisingly good, one or two of the ladies displaying quite admirable ball control, whilst combination was by no means a negligible quantity. Coulthard's were strongest in defence, the backs battling against long odds, never giving in, and the goalkeeper doing remarkably well, but the forwards, who were understood to have sadly disappointed their friends, were clearly afflicted with nerves.

All the conventions were duly honoured. The teams on making their appearance (after being photographed) indulged in 'shooting in', and the rival captains, before tossing the coin for choice ends, shook hands in the approved manner. At first the spectators were inclined to treat the game with a little too much levity, and they found amusement in almost everything from the pace, which until they got used to it, has the same effect as a slow-moving kinema picture, to the 'how-dare-you' expression of a player when she was pushed by an opponent.

But when they saw that the ladies meant business, and were 'playing the game' they readily took up the correct attitude, and impartially cheered and encouraged each side. Within five minutes Dick, Kerr's had scored through Miss Whittle, and before half-time they added further goals by Miss Birkens – a fine shot from 15 yards' out, just under the bar – and Miss Rance. Coulthard's, who were quite-out of the picture in the first half, 'bucked up' after the interval, and deserved a goal, but it was denied them, much to the disappointment of the spectators. They had a rare opportunity from a penalty in the last few minutes, but the ball was kicked straight at the keeper. On the other hand, Dick, Kerr's added to their score, Miss Rance running through and netting whilst the backs were 'argafying' about some alleged offence, a natural touch which greatly delighted the onlookers. Mr. John Lewis plied the whistle with discretion, whilst keeping within the four corners of the law, though he was clearly in a dilemma, probably for the first time in his official career, when one of the players was 'winded' by the ball.

In addition to the shift in attitudes and the charity element, what is notable from this report is that the women's teams actually impressed in sporting terms, too. It is impossible to say whether that shift in attitudes was simply the result of the watching press and public being more receptive to actually watching the football rather than the women themselves, or whether a more modern society was just better able to context-ualise the match. Either way, the praise was overwhelmingly positive and the match would kick-start a dynasty. Unlike the pre-war attempt at establishing women's football, the Dick,

Kerr Ladies and other factory teams would not fade away but instead become popular and powerful enough to rattle the footballing establishment.

In fact, Frankland's team would continue to play until 1965, outlasting the manager himself, two world wars and a Football Association clampdown on women's football and all that would flow from it.

4 – Charity

At the close of the war, the significant social impact made by women started to translate into the political field. Prime Minister David Lloyd George praised the contribution that women workers had made, saying: 'It would have been utterly impossible for us to have waged a successful war had it not been for the skill and ardour, enthusiasm and industry which the women of this country have thrown into the war.'

Laws started to change. In 1918 the Representation of the People Act came in, giving the vote to men over twenty-one regardless of whether they owned property, and women over thirty who met certain property requirements (or whose husbands did). That gave the vote to some 8.4 million women (around two in five), but the overwhelming majority of working-class women, who had given so much to the war effort, were still excluded from participating in the country's democratic processes. It would take another ten years before the age limit on women voters was reduced to twenty-one and the property restrictions were lifted.

The Parliament (Qualification of Women) Act followed later in 1918 and allowed women over the age of twenty-one – weirdly below the age at which they could vote – to stand for election to Parliament. The first woman to do so was Irish revolutionary Constance Markievicz, who was elected while in Holloway Prison for her part in the Easter Uprising of 1916. As a Sinn Féin MP she abstained from taking up her seat in the UK Parliament, instead becoming the first female cabinet minister in Europe as a part of the first Dáil (Irish parliament). In the same year Christabel Pankhurst narrowly missed out on being elected, while in 1919, Nancy Astor would be the first woman to take her seat in the House of Commons, representing the Conservative Party.

The Sex Disqualification (Removal) Act of December 1919 ruled that people could not be discriminated against on the basis of their sex for jobs in the civil or judicial service. Despite these political changes, women still faced many challenges. With the men returning from the front lines, the number of women workers fell back to pre-war levels as they were forced out of the workplaces. Winston Churchill, then minister of munitions, disgracefully praised munitions firms for 'commendable promptitude in immediately dismissing several thousands of their women workers' before being forced to hold back on further lay-offs after a backlash that 'recoiled on my head and caused a great deal of unfavourable comment'.

The findings of a government report into women's wages, following strikes of British workers likely inspired by revolutionary events in Russia, were released after the war. The report was favourable to the idea of equal pay for equal work and the trade unions were given guarantees that either sex doing the same skilled work would be paid the same. However, women were still viewed as being the weaker sex generally, so weren't considered to be doing equal work, thus providing loophole after loophole to employers.

In the US things were changing too, albeit at a slower pace due to the physical distance of the country from the front lines – meaning fewer women were needed to fill the gaps left by travelling soldiers – and the country's late involvement, having only joined the war effort in 1917.

Activist Margaret Sanger had opened the first birth control clinic in 1916 in Brooklyn and was promptly arrested for providing information on contraception, for which she was sentenced to thirty days in a workhouse. In 1918 she won a lawsuit which would exempt doctors from the law that prohibited the distribution of information on birth control. Her clinics would eventually become Planned Parenthood, the prominent charity that provides sexual healthcare in over 600 clinics today.

Women gained the right to vote in the US shortly after, with the passing of the Nineteenth Amendment in 1920 after years of protests, hunger strikes and incarcerations (although African American and Native American women would remain disenfranchised until the Voting Rights Act of 1965). Following this victory for suffrage the Women's Joint Congressional Committee was founded, representing up to twelve million women. That body forced through the introduction of an act ensuring that federal funding would be used to help the new workforce of women with maternity and childcare. It was revolutionary. Prior to its implementation health programmes had been primarily brought in on a state-by-state or local basis. However, a mere nine years after its introduction the act was allowed to lapse, seen as too radical for a country that has long baulked at the idea of universal state-funded healthcare.

By 1923 the first version of the Equal Rights Amendment which said that 'men and women shall have equal rights

47

throughout the United States and every place subject to its jurisdiction' was introduced. Women needed to work and they needed to be paid properly. They still do, almost a century later, but this was thrown into particularly sharp relief at the time as there was a huge increase in the number of single women in Europe who had to be their own breadwinners, due to a whole generation of men having been lost in the war. Whatever the challenges they continued to face, these women had been empowered by their wartime efforts – and they were not going to leave the football pitches or relinquish their new-found strength easily.

The women of teams such as Dick, Kerr Ladies were no exception. The charity efforts of women's teams had raised thousands and, as word of their skill and fundraising abilities got around, they were inundated with requests from across the country to come and play. In 1921 the Preston-based Dick, Kerr Ladies played sixty-seven games and had to turn down a slew of requests for further fundraising matches. Charities, hospitals, mayors and others all knew that the Dick, Kerr Ladies pulled the biggest crowds, and by extension the most money. They had the power to make a meaningful difference with their football, just as their work had made a meaningful difference as the war raged. During the war and in the immediate aftermath the focus was on supporting the war wounded.

Before the introduction of the National Health Service in 1948 healthcare for the working classes was primarily paid for through national insurance deductions from pay cheques, with services run by voluntary contribution schemes, charities and local authorities. However, this didn't cover the dependents of workers and meant that women and children requiring medical attention had to be paid for as and when needed, and many families struggled to afford it. The First and Second World Wars highlighted the inadequacies of healthcare and prompted women's teams' fundraising efforts. But the wars had also fuelled a desire for social change, for a society and systems that could provide a good standard of living for a population that had fought for the country. Churchill's Tories voted against the formation of a national health service twenty-one times, and it was the election of Clement Attlee's Labour Party in 1945 that eventually led to the founding of the NHS, a free-at-the-point-of-use service funded by general taxation.

Charity played an important role prior to the birth of the NHS, and women's football did its part, and it is impossible to say where the money raised by the women's game would have gone had the game's progress not been halted, as we'll discuss further, but what prompted people to show up in their droves for these charity games? It was partly down to the novelty of women's football, as we have already described. An article from the *Barnet Press* in November 1921 satirised the way in which some enterprising clubs were making full use of this novelty factor to grow attendances and interest in the women's game. The report details an extraordinary list of rules for the – presumably apocryphal – Barnet Blazers' Ladies' Football Club:

> *1. That this club shall consist exclusively of ladies, and that no one beneath a fine etcher shall be admitted.*

2. *That blue silk knickerbockers and blouses shall be worn, but not shin-guards, as they are unbecoming.*

3. *That preference shall be given to tall ladies of good figure, as they will look best in club photographs, and will be more likely to attract a good gate.*

4. *That all members who are weak in footwork be taken in hand by the trainer.*

5. *That the game to be played shall be Association, as the collaring in the Rugby game will disarrange our hair, and thereby often spoil a good match.*

6. *That any player guilty of making nasty satirical remarks on the play of members of her own side, such 'Kitty's miskick,' 'Puss in boots,' 'Let her slide,' etc., shall be suspended unless she has paid subscription.*

7. *That all corner kicks be taken from the midfield circle.*

8. *That the goalie must not do her hair up in the net.*

9. *That although all players should jump out of his way on the field of play, none are debarred from claiming a leap year privilege from a handsome referee after the game.*

10. *That when one player is going to give the ball a kick it shall be unladylike for any other player to interfere with her or to spoil her shot.*

11. *That it shall be unfair as well as unladylike for a side to kick two goals running. Each side shall be allowed to kick in turn, to avoid the suspicion of unfairness.*

12. *That all players who are not on the ball shall stand in graceful attitudes, and wear half-tone expression on their faces.*

13. *That there shall be no play if it rains.*

14. *That if the ball gets very dirty it shall be sent by special*

*messenger to the 'Old Dutch Laundry' to be washed, and
play suspended until its return.*

15. *That tea shall be served every ten minutes, and cream
chocolates during the interval at half-time.*

16. *That every member shall look her best on match days. Paper
patterns of stylish knickerbockers and pretty blouses may be
obtained from the club captain.*

17. *That all eligible bachelors in Barnet be supplied with the
club's match card, and asked to attend and improve the
plate.*

Beyond sheer novelty, however, the suspension of the professional men's leagues also meant that football fans were hungry for the game, for any football on offer. The war had had a huge impact on community feeling too: everyone had pulled together to help the war effort and that ethos did not die at its close.

'The novelty of it would have probably been the initial lure, then it was about patriotism as well. People in Britain had a tendency to all stick together when the chips are down; as a community, everybody pulled together,' says Gail Newsham.

So the crowds kept turning out and the women kept playing. Predictably, the more they played the better they got and the appreciation for the teams grew from just being about the money they were raising to also being about their skills on the field.

'I remember interviewing an old guy when I first started my research back in the 1990s, and he'd been at the night match [a match played by searchlight in 1920], and he could even remember the captain's name, the player he thought was the most outstanding, which was Alice Kell,' says Newsham. 'I was staggered by the fact that after all these years he still remembered how good they were. Another guy that I spoke to who'd watched them in the 1920s said he went to watch because: "I wanted to see a good game of football." It wasn't about gender or seeing women in shorts; it was just a desire to watch some good football.'

And Dick, Kerr Ladies certainly provided that. On 1 September 1921 the *Derby Daily Telegraph* reported on a match against Coventry under the headline 'From Fun to Cheers'. Fans 'began to look at things from a different viewpoint when Lily Parr tricked her way, by deft footwork, past a couple of defenders and shot the ball goalwards with surprising force'. The team would raise over £600 (approximately £30,000 today) for the Mayor's Hospital Fund, including £37 (£1,850) from the sale of the match ball. These were big amounts of money.

On 6 September, the *Dundee Evening Telegraph* wrote of the Dick, Kerr Ladies team that 'by then they had raised £47,000 (the equivalent of almost £2.4 million today) for those in need'. The report went on:

Lily Parr, the sixteen-year-old outside left, can boot a ball further than any lady in the country. The whole of the team excel in several branches of sport, such as running, jumping, swimming, tennis, hockey, and boxing. Miss Walker and Miss Woods have remarkable times for the 100 yards sprint. The team are proud holders of six silver cups and two sets of gold medals. They are also proud of their record in many ways:

1. *Going through a whole season without defeat.*
2. *The record number of goals scored; last season, 395.*
3. *The record small number of goals scored against them;
   16 last season.*

Parr and her contemporaries – whose impact as individuals we will discuss further along – became household names. The potent goalscorer has become the unofficial figurehead of the team but she was by no means the solo star. Florrie Redford was even more deadly in front of goal, while Frankland had persuaded French star Carmen Pomiès to stay in England and join the team after a tour of France in 1921.

Eventually, with the war over, women's teams broadened the scope of the causes they backed. After the coal industry was re-privatised on 1 April 1921 (having been nationalised during the war) miners were locked out of work for refusing to accept wage cuts. The 'lock out' would last three months and mining communities struggled to put food on the table as their bosses attempted to starve them back to work. Dick, Kerr Ladies, and other teams, would shift their fundraising efforts to these devastated communities, in towns and cities which many of the players came from. Frankland's side would travel to play in key mining cities such as Swansea, Cardiff and Kilmarnock.

By 1925 the *Kilmarnock Herald and North Ayrshire Gazette* reported that: 'The Dick, Kerr girls have a wonderful record both in playing and in raising funds for charitable objects. To date, they have raised the magnificent sum of £83,000 for ex-servicemen's organisations, hospitals etc. Miss Lily Parr,

outside left, is a really amazing player and would undoubtedly be playing First League if the English football legislators
would permit it.'

That £83,000 would be equivalent to over £5.16 million
today – a truly phenomenal level of fundraising. The growing
sums of money the teams were able to pull in, and the causes
they were supporting, would begin to draw the attention of
those in charge of the game and the ruling elite generally, not
always with favourable results. Money was pouring in from
football fans that they had no control over, it was going to
causes they often did not support and it provoked a rabid
response that would push the development of the women's
game back further than anyone at the time could have likely
imagined.

5 – The ban

Despite women having been turfed out of the workplaces in large numbers and the return of men's football following its suspension between 1915 and 1919, the women's game was thriving at the turn of the 1920s, with the Dick, Kerr Ladies at the forefront.

In 1920 the team would play four international home fixtures against a French team led by women's sport advocate Alice Milliat, at Deepdale, at Stockport, in Manchester and then at Stamford Bridge. The team then headed to France and played in Paris, Roubaix, Le Havre and Rouen. It would prove to be a hugely popular tour and on the team's return to England, the hype ahead of a scheduled Boxing Day match against rivals St Helens at Everton's Goodison Park was building. Few though could have predicted the seismic impact that the impending fixture would have on the future of women's football.

On the day of the match a staggering 53,000 fans would file into the ground for the game with, according to the diary of player Alice Stanley, a further 10–15,000 supporters turned away from the at-capacity ground. It set an attendance record that would not be surpassed for ninety-two years – until Team GB beat Brazil at Wembley during the London 2012 Olympics in front of 70,584 – and remains the biggest domestic game in the history of women's football in England, with the 38,262 that watched Arsenal defeat

Tottenham at the new Tottenham Hotspur Stadium on 17 November 2019 at number two.

It reportedly broke another record too, with the *Lancashire Evening Post* on 28 December 1920 saying: 'The most remarkable "gate" of the holiday, however, was at Goodison Park yesterday morning [Boxing Day] where the Dick, Kerr ladies beat St. Helens ladies 4–0 in a match on behalf of the unemployed and disabled ex-service men. The attendance was estimated at 53,000 and the receipts were over £3,000 exclusive of tickets. This being an easy record for a charity match in England.'

The money raised that day was the equivalent of around £140,000 today. This focused the minds of those watching the Dick, Kerr Ladies and other women's teams with mistrust and trepidation. In fact, it would be this hugely successful match that would trigger the devastation of the women's game.

The FA and the political establishment were not blind to the growing popularity and success of women's football. The huge sums of money that were being raised were outside their jurisdiction and control. Worse still, that money was no longer being raised to support the war wounded but was being channelled into political and working-class causes – causes antithetical to the establishment.

So, one year after over 53,000 spectators turned out to watch at Goodison Park, the FA voted to ban women's football. The sport's governing body did not have the power to ban women from playing outright – that was impossible, so instead they ruled that women's games were barred from FA-affiliated football grounds.

The FA's Consultative Committee's ruling stated:

Complaints having been made as to football being played by women, Council felt impelled to express the strong opinion that the game of football is quite unsuitable for females and should not be encouraged.

Complaints have also been made as to the conditions under which some of the matches have been arranged and played, and the appropriation of receipts to other than charitable objects. The Council are further of the opinion that an excessive proportion of the receipts are absorbed in expenses and an inadequate percentage devoted to charitable objects.

For these reasons the Council requests the Clubs belonging to the Association refuse the use of their grounds for such matches.

They were scared and so they acted before it progressed further. 'The women's football movement was spreading more rapidly in the North than in the South. Steps had already been taken in Lancashire and Yorkshire to found a league. A national association was also being spoken of,' said the *Leeds Mercury* on 7 December.

'Of course the Football Association's objection to women's football is not confined to the question of allotting gate receipts. Women's football is entirely unaffiliated – no government exists for it. And there is a general feeling that football is no game for women. It is too strenuous, that being the view of many famous specialists,' said the *Sheffield Daily Telegraph* on 9 December.

Interestingly, this was not the first time the FA had attempted to place restrictions on the game. In the 1890s the

FA Council sent warnings to clubs about the use of their grounds for ladies' football matches. In 1902 the FA passed a motion which banned mixed-sex games, but there is also some evidence pointing to this ban having extended to women's teams' use of FA-affiliated grounds too. Whether this is true, and if so, whether it was ever properly enforced or formally lifted, is unclear. However, there are references that imply it was still in place as far as 1917. *Sporting Life* on 13 November 1909 reported that 'ladies football teams are under the ban of the Football Association,' while in the 31 March 1917 *Star Green 'Un* sports special (a sports newspaper in Sheffield that was published on Saturday evenings), it was stated that 'the F.A. rule forbidding the use of their club grounds for ladies' football matches is still in existence'. The presence of such 1902 restrictions would perhaps offer an explanation for the tailing off of the game after its run of popularity in the late nineteenth century.

Regardless of whether the ban in 1902 similarly denied the use of FA-affiliated grounds, it did not stop the resurgence of women's football during the war and it is almost impossible to believe that this increased visibility, culminating in the 53,000 spectators at Goodison Park, did not act as a significant contributing factor to the new ban of 1921.

Newsham's opinion is that the record-breaking Boxing Day match of 1920, which followed games watched by over 35,000 at Old Trafford and 25,000 at Deepdale, was instrumental.

I think the Goodison match would have sent a seismic shock throughout the football world, because so many people went to that match. We must remember that in 1920 they'd expanded

the men's leagues – there was a new Division Three, North and
South – so they had practically doubled the amount of clubs and
all these people are going to watch women's football as opposed
to men's football. There was obviously going to be a conflict at
some stage, wasn't there? The Goodison match acted as a wake-up
call. That was Boxing Day 1920. The FA then started stepping in
to make it more difficult for clubs to let the grounds to women's
teams. Teams and clubs had to supply statements of accounts after
every game and they couldn't play without permission from the
FA. They were putting obstacles in the way throughout 1921. Then
came 5 December, when they dealt the fatal blow and banned
them from playing anyway.

The players were furious. 'When I spoke to Alice Norris [one
of the Dick, Kerr players of the time] and some of the other
ladies they all said they thought that the FA was just jealous because they were getting bigger crowds,' Newsham says.
'Obviously they were devastated. Everybody knows how much
work the women did during the war, all the hard work, the
manual jobs, everything that they did, so it didn't stack up.'

Reports of the ban were mixed. On one side, papers like
the *Hull Daily Mail* delighted in the ban and praised the FA.
Their report gives a fascinating insight into just how powerful and influential football and its governing agency were in
British society at the time, which offers a stark glimpse at
the effect the ban could have on the position of women in
society more generally:

It is an excellent thing that the Football Association has
considered the question of women playing football. The 'F.A.' is

*really a sort of Venetian oligarchy in the best sense of the word.
It is 'a pyramid of Soviets' – again in the best sense of the word;
and we make bold to say that its rule and governance of its
great game is a pattern and an example to all legislative bodies,
Parliament not excepted. This Council is so wise that its decisions
are respected universally, and its prestige so high that disobedience
never enters the minds of its associates and followers.*

*It can bind and loose, make or mar, suppress or exalt, and
it controls not only the game, the clubs, the officials, and the
players, but the crowd, too – and even the crowd fears it. This
august body has decreed that women's football is undesirable. It
is a game 'not fitted for females.' It discourages its clubs offering
or selling the use of their grounds. It deplores the fact that in
some cases so large a share of the 'gate' receipts have gone in
'expenses.' All this is a pretty big mouthful for women's clubs
and the public to be going on with! We are not in the least
enamoured of women's football.*

Others gave space for the players to have their say. Dick,
Kerr Ladies' captain Alice Kell, who was described in the
press as an 'unassuming, intelligent working girl', said:

*We girls play football in a proper spirit. We do not retaliate if
we are bowled over, and we show no fits of temper. We are all
simply amazed at the action of the authorities in placing a ban
upon the sport we love with all our heart. Surely to goodness
we have the right to play any game we think fit without
interference from the Football Association! We are all working
girls dependent upon our weekly wages and living with our
parents and others partly dependent upon us.*

By the 150 matches we have played we have raised over £60,000 for ex-service men's funds, hospitals and infirmaries. Not a single penny piece have we been paid as remuneration. All we have relied on above our railway fares and hotel expenses is the amount of wages we should have earned had we been working.

During the darkest hours of the war we provided, despite the scoffers who have never seen us play, healthy sport for those who were not actually engaged in the conflict.

We have been playing for nearly seven years, and my accident is the first that has occurred to any of our girls. We do not require toilet cream, powder puffs, eyebrow pencils, lip salve, and other aids to beauty. Our complexions are our own, given to us by nature and our activities in the open air.

We shall find some means to carry on. Letters of sympathy are pouring in from all parts of the country.

However, the great and the good came out to applaud the FA and condemn the existence of the women's game. The manager of Tottenham at the time, Peter McWilliam, said that he was 'convinced the Football Association is right'.

'I have seen one or two women's matches, and these have left me convinced that the game can only have injurious results on the women,' he said. Arsenal manager Leslie Knighton agreed: 'Anyone acquainted with the nature of the injuries received by men footballers could not help but think – looking at girls playing – that should they get similar knocks and buffetings, their future duties as mothers would be seriously impaired.'

Doctors also jumped in to voice their support for the decision. Harley Street physician Dr Mary Scharlieb said:

'I consider it a most unsuitable game; too much for woman's physical frame.' Meanwhile an unnamed doctor who reportedly worked in football professionally told a *Lancashire Daily Post* representative that 'from every point of view it was undesirable that girls should play such a strenuous game as football'. The report continued:

> *He has himself had to attend three girl footballers who had been affected internally by playing. And he is convinced that physiologically it was most harmful, whilst the risks were very much greater than in the case of men players.*
>
> *He does not believe that women are fitted for violent leg strain, and that even professional dancing on stage, which, of course, is not associated with the same dangers from external causes as football, is objectionable on this account. The periodicity of a woman's life and their delicate organism emphasises the danger of accident, strain, and the ordinary risks of violent exertion. As a spectacle, too, he does not think it at all satisfactory, but only attractive as a novelty, so that when this phase has passed he thinks people will realise that it was not nice to see girls taking part in the strenuous practices of the football field.*

The then FA secretary, Frederick Wall, who took the job in 1895, had also seemingly made up his mind on women's football long before the ban came in. In his autobiography *50 Years of Football 1884–1934*, he said: 'I was asked to referee the first women's football match at Crouch End. I declined, but I went to see the match and came to the conclusion that the game was not suitable for them. Someone declared that one of the players was a "Tommy" made up as a woman. The Football Association have discouraged this invasion of the "eternal feminine," just as they have discountenanced Sunday Football.'

There were dissenting voices in the FA Council meeting that would choose to implement a ban, however. One came in the form of a statement read to the committee by Major Cecil Kent from Liverpool, a former honorary secretary of Old Westminsters FC. In his statement, Major Kent said that he had attended around thirty women's football matches and pointed out that the women's game had contributed £100,000 to charity in two years while the FA's charity matches had only contributed about £20,000 to deserving causes each year (the FA replied that this was misleading and only accounted for practice matches played in August).

'On all hands I have heard nothing but praise for the good work the girls are doing and the high standard of their play,' he added. 'The only thing I now hear from the man is the street is "why has the FA got their knife into girls' football?" What have the girls done except to raise large sums for charity and to play the game? Are their feet heavier on the turf than the men's feet?'

The captain of the Strand Corner House Women's Football Team, a Miss A. Long, would also give an impassioned defence of the game to the room. 'In my experience of women's football matches,' she said, 'I do not remember any serious injury to any of the players. I recollect one broken arm. But accidents happen in all games. What people forget is that women footballers play women and not men. Our girls are a wonderfully healthy lot and thoroughly enjoy the game. We sacrifice our holidays for the game and for the sake of charity.'

It was also reported in the *Lancashire Evening Post* that 'of the sportsmanship of the girls there can be no question. One of Dick, Kerr's best players is a nurse at the Whittingham Lunatic Asylum. Recently she was on duty all night in charge of refractory patients. When she came off duty she cycled seven miles in the wet to Preston, travelled by train to the Midlands, played a fine game in the afternoon before a record crowd and was back on duty at the Whittingham late the same night.' The article continued later:

The organisers of the ladies' clubs, of whom Mr. A. Frankland, Dick, Kerr's honorary secretary, is a fine type, give all their spare time without any return. For four years Mr. Frankland has given up every Saturday afternoon and many another day as well, while every Sunday he has many hours of writing, and so far he has not even received a single memento of his great work.

The girls are all workers, and it is only by the sportsmanship of their various employers they get time off for football. Naturally, however, they are not paid by their firms when they are away, and all they get from the large 'gates' which they draw is the equivalent called 'loss of time' to what their firm would have paid them if they had been working, generally not more than 10s. for a whole day.

Personally I really can see no reason why they should not be well paid, for, if they did not play, the charities, instead of receiving large sums, would get nothing at all. But the girls never dream of making such a request and the fact remains that they are not paid except for 'loss of time'.

I have often heard it suggested that the F.A. objected because the girls were entertained to lunch and tea after travelling a hundred miles. This point is almost too childish to answer for I suppose even male professional players have a meal sometimes.

It is perhaps a little off-piste to add, but there was some dark irony to be found in the *Yorkshire Post and Leeds Intelligencer*'s coverage of the news of the ban. Below a report headlined 'Drastic Action by Football Association Council' was an article reporting on the death of Keighley men's forward Patrick Joseph Collins mid-game, under the headline and subheads: 'Keighley Footballer's Death at Batley. Sad Result to Strenuous Game. A Victim of Over-exertion.'

While the Dick, Kerr Ladies played on far beyond the ban, as others, such as Heys from Bradford and Huddersfield Atlanta, did too, the effect of the ban was devastating because it extinguished the crowd sizes in an instant. Teams were forced into parks and friendly rugby or athletics clubs, but the stadium capacity offered by men's football clubs could not be matched. Without the opportunity for the masses to watch games regularly in large-capacity venues the interest naturally waned.

'What drives me mad is the injustice of it,' says Newsham. 'Imagine saying to Kelly Smith, or Megan Rapinoe, or any of the players today: "That's it, you're not playing anymore, you're banned. Nobody's going to remember it, whatever you've done, it doesn't matter, nobody is going to care or re-member." Imagine that. You can't imagine how they would feel, can you? But that's what happened to them.'

The English FA was far from the only national association to place restrictions on women's football during this period. In France women's football was banned from 1932 until 1975. In Spain the federation (RFEF) would deny women the right to play football from 1935 until 1980. Meanwhile in Brazil, a law was introduced in 1941 decreeing that women could not take part in a number of sports because 'violent' sports were 'not suitable for the female body'. It wouldn't be lifted until 1981.

In 1955 the German Football Federation (DFB) in West Germany declared that women's football was 'essentially alien to the nature of women' and that 'in the fight for the ball, the feminine grace vanishes, body and soul will inevitably suffer harm'.

6 – Fifty years in the wilderness

Women's football took a big hit in 1921, but it did not die. Teams including Dick, Kerr Ladies continued, and others would also pick up the baton.

There was an attempt to bring together the 150-odd women's teams playing in 1921 and organise collectively, with the English Ladies' Football Association set up on 10 December 1921 at a meeting in Liverpool, with around thirty of the sides represented. At a second meeting, with the attendance doubled, teams agreed that pitch sizes would be changed, a lighter ball would be used, 'charging' (barging) would be banned and the use of hands would be allowed to protect faces. The ELFA also held a cup competition that was won by Stoke Ladies in June 1922. However, the organisation would only last one year as games and teams started to dwindle.

Undeterred, several teams persevered through the early years of the ban, seeking new opportunities to play the game they loved. Dick, Kerr Ladies were once more at the forefront of this movement, and in 1922 travelled to North America for the first time in their history, seeking new shores on which to play.

Although the FA's influence on their Commonwealth counterparts would see a planned Canadian tour cancelled while Dick, Kerr Ladies were en route, the US proved more welcoming. Initially the team was scheduled to take part in over twenty games throughout Canada and the US but upon arrival in Quebec the team were told that the Canadian FA did not sanction women's football and as a result they would be unable to play in the country. Though the development of the women's game had been slower to take hold in the US than in the UK, there is evidence, documented by historian Jean Williams in *A Beautiful Game: International Perspectives on Women's Football*, to suggest that women's football was played in the United States as early as 1918 and was more widely prevalent in colleges from the 1920s and thirties.

However, on arrival in the US, Dick, Kerr Ladies were scheduled to play nine games against men's teams across the country due to a lack of women's teams. The first of these was against Paterson FC in Clifton, New Jersey, on 24 September, in which the Preston-based team lost 6–3 in front of 5,000 spectators. Further games followed in Rhode Island, a 4–4 draw with J&P Coats Football Club, and New York City, a 7–3 defeat to Centro-Hispano in front of 7,000 fans, before a fixture on 8 October against Washington Soccer Club at the American League Park, which would also finish 4–4. There was significant interest in the local press around this game, with the *Washington Herald* describing it as 'one of the most unique international athletic competitions in the history of District Sportsdom', and the *Washington Post* reporting on the match, which took place in front of some 7,000 fans:

The fair kickers of the Dick, Kerr's women's soccer club of Preston, England, lived up to their reputation yesterday at American League Park when they battled the Washington soccer eleven to a 4 to 4 draw. The women showed a fairly good dribbling game, but their kicking lacked both speed and force. The Washington kickers were extended most of the way. Although the men players through good teamwork were given many opportunities they were not successful in registering goals, due to the brilliant defense of Miss Carmen Pomies, the Preston goalkeeper. She checked eleven of the fifteen attempts made by the local booters. Miss Lily Parr, at outside left, put up an aggressive game registering two goals in seven tries she had at the net. The girls were able to penetrate the Washington right wing with success, but were checked several times on attempts at the left wing and midfield. The District kickers counted first, Green placing one past Miss Pomies after 26 minutes of play. Miss Parr evened it up shortly before half time. The second half was rather loosely played by both clubs, but the women showed to better advantage with teamwork.

The women's team clearly impressed on their Stateside tour. Paterson goalkeeper Peter Renzulli, who played against them in New Jersey, said, 'We were national champions and we had a hell of a job beating them.' The *Fall River Evening Herald* in Massachusetts was similarly struck, stating that the team was 'one of the biggest things in soccer ever to have visited the United States'.

Back in the UK, matches may have been harder to come by, but Dick, Kerr (renamed the Preston Ladies in 1926) pushed on regardless. By the 1930s they were still attracting thousands to games under their new name, and a 1931 report showed women's football, when it was played, was as attractive as ever:

In spite of the FA ban, women's football, which has been revived, seems to have lost little of its popularity. Mr. Alfred Frankland, who has been connected with the sport from its inception, believes it would still draw crowds and raise thousands for charity on proper grounds, and considers they are entitled to 'fair play from the FA'.

Alice Kell (now Mrs. Cook) and Florrie Haslam, two members of the original Dick, Kerr's ladies football team, watched their successors, Preston Ladies, play in a charity match at Stockport the other night. Miss Haslam considers football a grand health-giving game for girls, and not as big a strain on the physique as tennis.

The players got as much fun out of the game as any of the 5,000 spectators, especially the tiniest and perhaps most active girl on the field, Miss Yates, whom her friends call 'Glaxo'. She stands a few inches less than five feet, a golden-haired bundle of energy and smiles, who took everything in excellent part.

As had been the case in the US, they also attracted the attention of men's players of the day. 'Amongst those who watched the Preston Ladies' FC defeat a side of French and English girls were Jasper Kerr, North End's left back, and Billy Bocking, the former Stockport County back who is now with Everton. Perhaps picking up points? Both were impressed with the promising exhibition of a sturdy 16-year-old girl full back on the Preston side, E. Clayton.'

In 1938, a year before the Second World War would up-end things once more, the *Western Morning News* reported a huge attendance at another Preston Ladies game:

There was a gate of 8,000, the largest for many years, at Hayes (Middlesex) Football Club ground this evening to see Hayes United Ladies Football Club defeated by seven goals to one by the Preston Ladies' Football Club.

The Preston Ladies, who are the champions, have beaten teams in England, France, Scotland, Wales, Belgium, and the USA and Canada and have not lost a match since 1934. They have played 437 matches in the past 20 years, lost seven and drawn six.

It was staggeringly impressive that they were able to carry on. This came down to the tenacity of the women and their simple desire to play football. For many years after the ban, Frankland received letters from across the country from players desperate to try out for the team. The orchestrator of the Dick, Kerr/Preston juggernaut would pass away in 1957, having handed the reins over to Kath Latham two years prior due to his ill health, but going into the 1960s the team started to struggle to attract enough players. Having led the way for almost fifty years and through the harshest of conditions, finally the flow of players reduced to a trickle and the team was ultimately forced to fold in 1965. Agonisingly the team fell apart one year before England's men's team would lift the World Cup and inspire a swathe of girls to pick up the game and less than a decade before the ban was lifted.

'It's a tragedy really that they would fold before the ban was lifted, but nothing's forever, is it?,' reflects Gail Newsham. 'Kath didn't want them to end up being a let-down or not being able to fulfil their fixtures, or to let the charities down.

A WOMAN'S GAME

So she had to make the decision to call it a day and sadly that's what happened.

'Sometimes in life, something special comes along where none of us really know why something worked but it did. I think we just have to be grateful that we have that and we can look back on it and cherish and say how great they were.'

How were teams like Preston able to work around the ban? One tactic, which had been employed throughout the early history of the game, was to use the fact that they were playing charity matches to pressure the FA and county FAs' related governing bodies into sanctioning the games. This was highly effective, if not always popular among representatives of the men's game. In response to a February 1931 fixture between Preston Ladies and a 'rest of England' team in support of the British Legion, the secretary of the Derbyshire FA, Joseph Holmes, offered his forthright opinion: 'As the game is for charity, we are putting no obstacle in the way of the organisers, but as far as we are concerned it is not a football match at all.'

Preston Ladies were far from the only team to be playing. Bolton Ladies, Rutherglen Ladies, Edinburgh City Girls, Glasgow Ladies – a host of teams sprung up or fought on in the interwar years. Many would suspend play during the Second World War, though some didn't.

As had been the case between 1914 and 1918, following the outbreak of the Second World War women were called out of their homes and into the factories. This time, women aged between twenty and thirty were also able to join the armed forces, following the introduction of the 1941 National Service Act. Around 640,000 women would do so, while

72

others flew unarmed aircraft, served as nurses or worked behind enemy lines as part of special operations.

On the Home Front, women were back in the munitions factories as well as working as engineers, mechanics, air-raid wardens and bus, fire engine and ambulance drivers. By the middle of 1943 close to 90 per cent of single women and 80 per cent of married women were working in factories, on the land (80,000 joined the Women's Land Army) or in the armed forces.

The ban on women's football being played in FA-affiliated grounds was still in place and would not be relaxed at any point during the war, so female players were unable to capitalise on the pausing of men's football as they had done during the First World War. However, factory teams still formed and football was an important recreational activity for those that enlisted.

In June 1940, a women's team from Stirlingshire representing the Patons and Baldwins factory played a team from Cruikshank & Co, Ltd. In Portsmouth, women bus conductors from Hants and Dorset Motor Services were victorious in a game against the women bus drivers of the Provincial Omnibus Company. In Woking, teams representing Guildford M&S and Guildford Woolworths would play a mini tournament with a team from the Lion Works.

So even if the war did not enable the mass crowds that the factory teams had enjoyed some twenty-five years earlier, it did nonetheless encourage a new generation of women players. And at the close of the war in 1945, these women were united in looking for teams to join so they might continue enjoying their new pastime.

Bolton Ladies would become one of the premier teams in the post-war period. In 1945 they played an away match against the Edinburgh Lady Dynamos in front of 17,000 fans at Meadowbank. Shortly afterwards, however, the Scottish FA decreed that 'all grounds which allowed women's football would be banned' and the Edinburgh council refused a licence for a repeat fixture the following year, for fear of affecting Hearts or Hibernian men's teams.

Another of the most significant teams to rise to the fore in the middle of the ban would be the Manchester-based Corinthian Ladies Football Club. The Corinthians were formed in 1949 by Bolton Wanderers scout and referee Percy Ashley, who was motivated to create a team so that his partially deaf daughter had somewhere to play. Ashley's team would go on to build a legacy not too dissimilar to that of Dick, Kerr Ladies, and perhaps even more impressive given that they did it on the fringes, with the game outlawed from the biggest grounds.

Faced with a dearth of opponents, Ashley also founded a second team, known as the Nomads, for the Corinthians to play against. The two teams went on to tour the world over the next few years, playing in Germany in 1957, where they would win an unofficial (as Europe's governing body UEFA did not organise competitions for the women's game at this time) European Cup, Portugal in 1957, the Netherlands in 1959, in a hugely significant tour of South America and the Caribbean in 1960 and Italy in 1961. The teams would also play matches against Ireland, Wales, Morocco and France, winning over fifty trophies and raising a huge £275,000 for charity.

It is hard to overstate the importance of the Corinthians in post-war women's football. No other team managed to travel as extensively promoting women's football, hosting tournaments and raising money for charity during this period.

When people discuss the history of women's football today, there is often a huge gap, an assumption that we jumped from Dick, Kerr Ladies in the 1920s to the 1990s and the teams and formats we're more familiar with now. Often, the huge battling history of the women that fought on and played during the ban is a less well-known part of the journey. The Corinthians and other teams of the post-war years really fought against tradition and the establishment to be able to play. It would take a drawn-out, decades-long fight from women's teams – allied with a wider social backdrop that was shifting the dial in favour of greater gender equality overall – before the establishment recognised the damage done by the ban.

TWO

From the Ashes

7 – Lifted

By the late 1960s, the game was again drawing the attention of the FA – in fact, it was banging at the door, desperate for recognition. And this time the FA would not be able to sweep it aside.

After the Second World War the struggle for women's rights had stalled a little. During the war, subsidised day nurseries for working mothers had been set up and run by local councils and funded by the Ministry of Health. With the ceasefire this state-run childcare provision came to a close, making it harder for working women to stay working. In 1951, 75 per cent of adult women were (or had been) married, and even more specifically, 84.4 per cent of women between forty-five and forty-nine were married. Against this backdrop of a society with conservative views on women's place within it, the FA had, to some extent, been able to get away with ignoring the development of women's football.

By the 1960s and 1970s, however, following the lead of the US, second-wave feminism had reached the UK's shores, and gains were slowly being made. In 1961 the contraceptive pill was launched (although it wouldn't be available to unmarried women before 1976). In 1964 the Labour Party led by Harold Wilson secured a narrow victory in the general election over the Conservatives, ending thirteen years of Tory rule. The new government had edged into power on the basis of a manifesto that led on equality and on investment in social care and public services. The Wilson government would outlaw capital punishment and decriminalise homosexuality, and shortly after a snap election in 1966, which they won by a landslide, also introduced the 1967 Abortion Act, legalising abortion in the UK (excluding Northern Ireland).

The issue of equal pay was also forced back on the agenda, courtesy of the three-week strike of 850 female machinists at Dagenham's Ford factory in 1968. The women went on strike after a change to the factory's pay structure had reclassified them as unskilled workers, to be paid 15 per cent less than their male colleagues. With no one else able to make the car seat covers the 'unskilled' women expertly stitched, their industrial action brought production at the factory to a complete halt. The machinists' cause was taken up by Barbara Castle, the first – and, to date, only – woman to hold the office of first secretary of state, who struck a deal that would see the women's pay rise to 92 per cent of the wages of the men.*

That historic strike would lead to the founding of the National Joint Action Campaign Committee for Women's Equal Rights. This new group went on to hold an equal-pay protest on 18 May 1969 of 1,000 people; would inspire the 1970 strike of Leeds garment workers, where 20,000 women from forty-five factories marched against the low wage rise that had been accepted by their union; and

---

* It would take sixteen years, and further industrial action, before the female machinists were finally reclassified into the same skilled category as their male counterparts in 1984.

eventually triggered the introduction of the Equal Pay Act in 1970, which would make pay disparity and any difference in conditions of employment between men and women illegal.*

Alongside all of this social and political upheaval, women's football was growing in strength and popularity, despite the FA's historic efforts to squash it. By 1969 enough momentum had been generated for those involved in women's football to have another go at organising the game nationally. On 1 November that year forty-four women's teams would come together at Caxton Hall in London to found the Women's Football Association.

There, Arthur Hobbs, who five-time FA Cup winner Sue Lopez would describe in her book *Women on the Ball* as 'the father of women's football', was elected the first secretary of the organisation. Another key figure in the founding of the WFA was Patricia Gregory, who at nineteen years old had been inspired to play after watching Tottenham win the FA Cup in 1971. Gregory wrote a letter to her local paper and received numerous replies from women wanting to play. There was a snag, though, as after fifteen women had crammed into her parents' living room and agreed to form a team, Gregory asked the council about pitch hire facilities, only to be told of the ban on women's football.

Gregory's team, White Ribbon, wrote to the FA to ask if they could join a league and received a reply from the then

* It is important to point out, though, that with a median gender pay gap of 15.5 per cent in 2020, neither the 1970 legislation nor the Equality Act of 2010 which replaced it are enough on their own to stop a disparity in the wages and conditions of men and women at work.

secretary Sir Denis Follows on 21 July 1967 which said: 'I enclose herewith for your information a copy of the Council decision of December, 1921, which decision was confirmed by the Council in December, 1962. As the Football Association does not recognise ladies' football teams, I am unable to inform you of any League to which you could apply for Membership.'

Unperturbed, White Ribbon would travel up and down the country playing men's youth teams. Gregory's advert in a football magazine asking for teams to play against caught the eye of Arthur Hobbs, who invited White Ribbon to come and play in his eight-team tournament in Kent, and a key alliance was formed.

Six months after the first meeting to set up the WFA, seven regional leagues were present at the first annual general meeting of the body – the South East, Kent, the Midlands, Sussex, West Mercia, Northampton and Southampton.

No longer able simply to brush women's football under the rug, scared of the growing momentum of the women's game and under increasing pressure from UEFA, the FA responded with a new tactic: to bring the game under its wing to control and manage its growth as best it could.

'Women's football is spreading so rapidly that the men want to get it organised under the control of national associations,' warned the *Liverpool Echo*.

So far, our own Football Association has steered clear of having anything to do with girls. But if the experience of other European countries is any guide, the austere men of Lancaster Gate will have to think again – and quickly.

Women's football has developed with such speed throughout Europe that delegates of UEFA discussed it at top level recently. The views expressed ranged from a heartfelt cry by one delegate of 'may God have mercy on us' to an urgent plea to get the girls properly organised before they make a monkey out of a man's game.

It was decided to appoint a special committee under the chairmanship of vice-president Sándor Barcs to discuss the problems of affiliating women's football to the national associations. Women play in 22 European countries, at varying levels of competition, but only in eight countries is it controlled by the national association.

An international women's association has already staged a world championship and proposes a European Cup competition. But, hints UEFA darkly, 'behind it all are managers more interested in show business than sport.' European football authority wants to get a grip of this rapidly developing set-up.

This pressure helped give Follows, the momentum needed to push through the change – something, his daughter Maggie Ferris is keen to stress, he would have been in favour of.

'He was always campaigning about things; that was just part of what he was,' explains Ferris. 'And he was quite self-effacing; he never made a big deal of any achievement, apart from, well, he was pretty pleased about winning the World Cup,' she adds with a laugh.

Follows, who was in charge at the FA from 1962, presided over England's 1966 World Cup win and hid the Jules Rimet trophy under his bed after its recovery (it had been stolen from an exhibition in London in March 1966) until the final. It then went on display until he could take it to the Mexico World Cup in 1970 stowed in his briefcase. Having also been the general secretary of BALPA, the pilots' union, he spent over a decade working to clear the name of Captain James Thain, the pilot initially held responsible for the Munich air disaster in 1958.

At the end of 1969 Follows wrote to Hobbs and the WFA to inform them that the FA had agreed to 'rescind the council's resolution of 1921'. It was a hugely significant moment in the history of women's football in England and yet there was no big announcement, no fanfare and no official records of the historic moment. 'There was no flash of light or anything like that,' Gregory told the *Telegraph* in 2021. 'I wish I could tell you there was great excitement, but there wasn't. We just solved each problem as it came, one by one.' That there was no fuss made is indicative of the lack of commitment to women's football that came with the lifting of the ban. However, this momentous decision gave access to the fertile fields where women players could plant seeds of growth.

Lifting the ban on women's football was one of Follows's final acts before he left the FA. 'In a lot of domestic ways he was not capable at all,' remembers Ferris. 'He could just about do tea and toast or boil an egg but in some ways he was a real innovator. He was in his treatment of women. I found an old photograph of a 1930s committee that he was on at the university and a third of the people in the photograph are women. He had always worked with women in an equivalent role; he never expected women to be the underdogs.' Follows would be named an honorary life vice president of the WFA for his role in lifting the ban, something he and his family were very proud of.

Duly warned of the risk posed by an untethered women's game, the FA started to move in January 1970 and county FAs polled their members over a possible rule change. The *East Kent Times and Mail* reported that 'Kent's soccer clubs are being asked to vote for or against lifting the controversial ban on women's footballers that has stood since 1921. Results of the poll will be taken by the Kent County Football Association to the next FA Council meeting on January 19, when a decision whether or not to recognise women's football will probably be made.'

The article also pointed to the increasing problem that the FA had of girls finding ways to play regardless of the ban: 'Public parks in recent years have seen a rapid growth in the number of all-girl games . . . There are a number of Thanet girl teams operating in the East Kent League and more and more members of the opposite sex are becoming involved in football. Their champion is Deal carpenter Mr. Arthur Hobbs, who has fought an untiring battle against the FA ban.'

There were even some voices looking favourably upon the change, with Yugoslavia's Professor Mikelov Andreyivic telling UEFA 'that a women's body structure is ideal for soccer – perhaps better than a man's'. Although, he added that 'the ball should be lighter and the pitch smaller'.

The ban was lifted in 1970 with the first Women's FA Cup final played in May 1971, with Southampton beating Stewarton and Thistle 4–1, and, on 28 February 1972, the

FA went one step further by finally formally recognising the women's game for the first time. A ninety-two-strong council assembly met in London and accepted the proposals put to them by a joint meeting between the FA and the WFA. The meeting ruled 'that all clubs be affiliated to a Women's Football Association which shall be supervised and controlled within the National Association'.

In addition the FA agreed to set up a joint consultative committee with the WFA that would assist with the organisation of referee courses and would aid the connections with UEFA and FIFA.

However, the FA also made clear that they would not interfere in the day-to-day running of the women's game, which would be left to the WFA, would not be providing financial assistance to the women's game and stressed that mixed football was still a no-go.

'Women's lib has scored again. This time at Lancaster Gate,' hailed the *Daily Mirror*. 'The Football Association, that last sporting bastion of masculine prejudice which is 109 years old this October, has fallen at last, and now recognises there is such a thing as women's soccer.'

The move also received poignant praise from the 1966 World Cup final hat-trick hero Geoff Hurst, who described the lifting of the ban as 'a victory for common sense', adding 'girls play tennis at Wimbledon so why should not women's soccer at Wembley be as big an attraction?'

Hobbs, who was still secretary of the Women's FA, said: 'There are close on 5,000 women footballers in this country and this is a move to regularise their affairs. In fact, there is talk of an official World Cup to be organised next year . . .

and it would be nice if it could be held in England, where the game was born.'

And the manager of Southampton Ladies, Norman Holloway, argued for a Cup Final at Wembley, suggesting that women's soccer could help kill violence on the terraces. He said: 'I don't think the tough boys would get rough if they could be entertained by girls' football before League games.'

Interestingly, the comments of those involved in the women's game that had pushed for the change were welcoming but also laced with a palpable mistrust towards the body that had excluded women for so long. Women's football was still being played throughout the ban, so in practice the main effect of its lifting was simply that players could access affiliated pitches and referees. However, they were still amateur and ultimately reliant on clubs and administrators that had for so long told women that they were not welcome in the sport. Administrative change was not enough; it needed to be coupled with an active desire to change attitudes and embrace the game. Instead, the WFA was kept at arm's length, allowed to run the game but lacking the support afforded to men's football. Overcoming this hurdle would be key to the development of the newly sanctioned sport from this point onwards.

8 – Finding a way to play

The FA's lifting of the ban in 1970 was a turning point for the game, but women's football was by no means wholeheartedly embraced by the governing body from this point onwards. To say it was tolerated would be a more apt description. Professionalism, in many countries, was a world away and those with ambitions of carving a career from their game had to be creative in their search for paid football.

In the years following the lifting of the ban, however, a degree of professionalism for female footballers could be found in a potentially surprising place. While players in Italy today are confined to amateur status, unable to earn more than €30,000 per year before tax,* during the 1970s and 1980s the Italians led the way in providing some form of professionalism.

Women's football in Italy can be traced back to the 1930s, with the first women's team formed in Milan in 1933 by the Gruppo Femminile Calcistico. It was to be an unfortunately short-lived project, however, cut short by the Italian Olympic Committee pulling players towards athletics. The birth and death of many subsequent clubs and attempts to organise the sport followed, before the Federazione Italiana Calcio

---

* There have long been campaigns for a change to the law, and in June 2020 the Italian Football Federation finally announced the launch of 'a gradual project aimed at recognising professionalism, starting from the 2022–23 season'.

Femminile (FICF) was eventually formed in 1968 and a first championship was started, originally with nine teams – Ambrosiana, Cagliari, Fiorentina, Genova, Lazio, Napoli, Milano, Piacenza and Roma – rising to ten when Real Torino joined a year later.

Soon after, in November 1969, Italy hosted a four-team 'Turin tournament' featuring Italy, Denmark, England and France. Thanks to sponsorship by the drinks company Martini & Rossi, all the teams involved had their kit and equipment paid for, as well as all their travel and accommodation – a situation that would remain vanishingly rare in most female competitions for many years to come.

In 1970 the FICF's first attempt at an Italian league was wound up and the ten teams involved formed a new federation, the Federazione Femminile Italiana Giuoco Calcio (FFIGC), which would also host the first Coppa del Mondo. This would come to be known as the first unofficial World Cup, as teams, players, and other proponents of the women's game reacted to FIFA's reticence to host international competitions by picking up the slack and taking on the challenge themselves.

The final of the Coppa del Mondo competition was played in Turin, with Italy narrowly losing to Denmark in front of an impressive 40,000 fans. Undeterred, however, Italy would play host to international competition a further four times between 1984 and 1988 – this time through the Mundialito, or little World Cup, which drew similarly sizeable crowds. All those tournaments played a hugely significant role in the development of international competition in the women's game (not least in giving the US women's national team its international debut in 1985), but they also put Italian women's football on show to fans and players from across the globe.

Italy's semi-professional offering attracted players from across Europe. England and Southampton's Sue Lopez and her international teammate Dot Cassell were both among a cohort from England that would play in Italy – Lopez being the first England player to compete semi-professionally overseas when she joined Roma in 1971.

Meanwhile, Ireland's Anne O'Brien and Scotland's Edna Nellis and Rose Reilly were all poached from French side Reims by Lazio and ACF Milan respectively. During their time at Reims, Nellis, Reilly and former teammate Elsie Cook were banned from representing their country indefinitely by the Scottish Women's FA after they expressed criticism about the lack of support for women's football. In response, Reilly traded her national allegiance to Italy and went on to be voted the team's best player at the 1984 Mundialito. She scored thirteen times in twenty-two games for her adopted country and lifted eight Scudetti in twenty years in Italy. Corinthians player Jan Lyons was threatened with never being able to play for England when she gave up her job at the Midland Bank to go and play for Juventus in 1973. The Italian team had been beaten by Corinthians in the final of the 1970 Reims International Football Tournament, hosted by French side Reims, in which Lyons and player of the tournament Margaret Whitworth, who Juventus tried to recruit, competed. When Lyons moved to Italy for two seasons, Juventus paid for her accommodation and food.

The Danish forward Susanne Augustesen was another star who was drawn to the professionalism afforded by Italy in the early 1970s, winning five Scudetti and three Italian Cups over the course of her career and was the league's top scorer in eight different seasons. Meanwhile, Pia Sundhage, the current Brazil manager and former head coach of the US national team, spent one season in Italy as part of a decorated playing career, scoring seventeen goals for Lazio.

These were players at the very top of their game, who knew their talents deserved more. And while Italy was by no means the only country to be making great steps forward during this period,* the role it played in hosting numerous international competitions and in providing a degree of professionalism, thanks to sponsorships and commercial interests, thrust it to the top.

Throughout the history of the women's game, international competitions have always acted as a catalyst for growth. Determination, grit, courage and bloody-mindedness have enabled the sport to stagger forwards and grow quantitatively. But it is through international tournaments that growth has been accelerated and qualitative leaps forward have been made. Big tournaments bring eyes. Their scale forces media coverage. They play on a nationalist competitiveness that forces federations to invest for the sake of pride. They are showcases.

The triumph of the England men's team in the 1966

---

* By 1980 West Germany had 111,000 women playing football, with the first women's DFB Cup played in front of 35,000 fans in 1981, while Denmark had 26,000 players in 1980.

World Cup played an important part in helping trigger the drive for the ban in England to be lifted and an upswing in interest in women's football. Four years later, an unofficial women's football team would represent England at the 1970 Coppa del Mondo, despite the protestations of the FA and the ban still being in place.

The 1970 team was assembled by Harry Batt, a bus driver and secretary of the Chiltern Valley women's team who spoke five languages and was involved in the WFA early on. Batt's team drew big crowds in proper stadiums in Italy, beating West Germany 5–1 in the quarter-finals before going out 0–2 to the eventual winners, Denmark, in the semis – but nothing could have prepared them for what waited in Mexico at the second unofficial Women's World Cup in 1971.

Again, the tournament was small. Six teams made the finals: hosts Mexico plus England, Argentina, Denmark, France and Italy. Martini & Rossi were the sponsors once more, covering the costs of each team's travel, kits and accommodation, while local companies from Lagg's Tea to Nikolai Vodka also supported the tournament. The *Corriere dello Sport* reported that a colossal 100,000 people watched the opening game between Mexico and Argentina at the Azteca Stadium in Mexico City, while the final between the hosts and Denmark was played in front of 110,000 spectators.

The tournament had faced strong opposition from the Mexican Football Federation which, under pressure from FIFA, said it would fine clubs that granted the use of their grounds. The competition's organisers had to think creatively and work around the ban – fortunately, both Azteca in the capital city and the Jalisco Stadium in Guadalajara were privately owned, so the tournament was able to be held across the two venues.

Part of the reason that the organisers were able to pull off such a hugely successful competition despite opposition was their use of promotional methods that appear crass in the extreme when viewed through the more progressive lens of today. The games were almost billed as a sort of cabaret show, shamelessly piggybacking on the success of the men's World Cup the preceding year. The players wore hot pants and bright colours to show off their bodies, the goalposts were painted pink, women security guards, translators and other officials wore pink uniforms and players had their hair, make-up and false eyelashes done before talking to the press and meeting the rapt public after games.

The *New York Times* reported on the event under the headline 'Soccer Goes Sexy South of Border', writing:

The second women's world soccer championship Aug. 15–Sept. 5 promises to be something of a mixture between sports event and a beauty contest.

'We're really going to stress the feminine angle,' said Jaime De Haro, head of the organising committee. Women who play soccer are not muscular monstrosities, but generally pretty girls.

'It's a natural,' De Haro said. 'The combination of the two passions of most men around the world: soccer and women.'

This cheapening of women's football actually helped it take steps forward. In that same year, 1971, UEFA would establish a committee for women's football that was asked to plan a European competition for the women's game. Though this tournament would never come to be, with the committee disbanded seven years later, FIFA was also starting to look at the women's game with a modicum of interest rather than disdain. In Italy and Mexico the game had attracted sponsors and fans, and had exploited merchandising to the max. It was making money and they were eyeing the potential pie.

'After years of regarding women soccer players as something of a joke, the world's exclusively male official soccer organisations are now prepared to take them seriously,' said Reuters, in April 1972. 'A European Cup for women and ultimately a Women's World Cup seem now only a matter of time.'

However, there were modified rules in FIFA's vision for the women's game. 'The ball may be lighter, the field smaller and the duration of matches shorter. Moreover, the offense of "ungentlemanly conduct" will have to be replaced by another term – "unwomanly," "unladylike" or "unfeminine." The exchange of jerseys on the field between teams at the end of a match obviously will have to be abandoned,' Reuters reported.

This change in tone and attitudes from the European and global governing bodies of the game heaped pressure on countries where the game was still banned. FIFA had instructed its members to encourage women's teams and to offer them facilities, while UEFA set up what would ultimately prove to be a useless committee which aimed to examine the question of women's soccer and to study rules for it.

All of this was triggered by the events in Italy and Mexico

and by the determination of the women, many of whom were teenagers, who left their homes and everything they knew to travel around the world and into the unknown, driven by a passion for football.

For Batt's England team 'it was like going into the Tardis or to Narnia, being transported to a different world,' said midfielder Chris Lockwood, who was fifteen when she boarded the plane headed for Mexico. 'I don't think we knew what to expect. We had only played in the small qualifying tournament in Sicily, which was played on the park-type pitches we were used to.' The youngest player on the team was thirteen-year-old Leah Caleb, who would be compared to George Best in the press before she travelled to Mexico.

A huge reception welcomed Batt's England side at the airport. Photographers' flashbulbs stunned the players, hundreds of fans chanted and celebrated their arrival, while others showed up at the players' hotel, offering gifts and asking for autographs. It was a world away from home, where women's football was still played in parks and leisure centres.

The competition was tough: England would lose 4–1 to Argentina and 4–0 to Mexico in their group, and 3–2 to France in a fifth-place play-off. Striker Janice Barton, a nineteen-year-old bank clerk from Biggleswade, scored all three of England's goals, and was also sent off after her strike in the opening game for leaving the pitch to take off her shin pads.

'I got kicked on the ankle and my legs were giving me trouble,' she said. 'I went over to the sideline to take off my shin pads and the referee ruled that I had left the field without permission.'

The Argentinian side 'played really rough', according to Batt. 'The girls are bruised all over.' He feared there would be more bruising games to come: 'I watched the ladies of Italy and France last night on TV, it was more like a bullfight than a soccer match.'

That physicality was used back home to strengthen the argument against the game and it was front-page news. 'Fourteen battle-scarred British girl footballers came home last night from the wars of the Women's World Cup in Mexico,' said the cover story of the *Daily Mirror* next to a picture of two players on crutches walking through the airport.

Here are two of them, 19-year-old skipper Carole Wilson, on the left, and 16-year-old Yvonne Farr – each with a leg in plaster. The rest of the team and three reserves are also nursing injuries after unladylike matches against Mexico and Argentina. And after they landed at London Heathrow Airport, the players learned that they may be banned by the British Women's Football Association. The association says that the gory goings-on down Mexico way were 'degrading.' It has branded the World Cup competition and the self-appointed British team as unofficial and 'illegal.' Now any girls who want to play for teams affiliated to the WFA in Britain will have to be 'investigated.'

Batt was dismissive of the threat and refused to recognise any authority of the WFA over the women's game in England. The then president of FIFA, Sir Stanley Rous, got in on the act. He used the events in Mexico to delay an apparent change of heart over the viability of the women's game, saying:

> *I'm not surprised. I think anything could happen when ladies play football in Mexico. As a matter of fact I was thinking of rewriting the rules for the International Board, to include laws for women footballers – but in view of this I think it might be difficult. You couldn't classify this type of conduct as ungentlemanly. And unladylike is hardly a strong enough word to use. I'm only glad I wasn't the referee.*

His claim of being on the verge of 'rewriting the rules' held water. In March 1970 the world governing body had surveyed its member federations on the status of women's football in their countries. The first question asked: 'Does your federation officially recognise Football for women?' They received ninety replies and only twelve (Algeria, South Africa, Upper Volta [now Burkina Faso], Chinese Taipei, Singapore, Thailand, Guatemala, Jamaica, France, West Germany, Sweden and Wales) said they did. FIFA were slowly moving into gear, but Rous's response to the events in Mexico demonstrate that he was still only too willing to put distance between himself and the women's game. However, its rise on the international stage would soon prove impossible for even FIFA to ignore.

9 – The game goes official

Where the first wave of feminism of the late nineteenth and early twentieth centuries was born from the new freedoms brought by the Industrial Revolution, and focused on the fight for suffrage and increased opportunities for women, second-wave feminism was a reaction to women being thrust back into the home as caregivers, mothers and housewives following the end of the Second World War, and limited to nursing, teaching or secretarial roles in the workplace.

This second wave of the late 1960s and early 1970s was much wider in scope than the first, taking up issues such as sexuality, workplace rights, reproductive rights (including birth control), domestic abuse, sexual violence and harassment. Where first-wave feminism mainly tackled the legal barriers, this new wave took aim at the patriarchal culture of society much more broadly.

Though originating from the US, it was not confined there – feminist organisations and movements took up familiar issues across Europe and the wider world following a similar timeline. But it is perhaps in the US where the movement had the biggest impact from a sporting point of view, triggering a growth in women's sport and football in particular that would eventually see the country offering the best professional terms for players and lead to the US women's national team becoming the envy of world football.

The key to that growth was the introduction of Title IX in 1972. The Civil Rights Act of 1964, initially proposed by President John F. Kennedy the preceding year, six months before his assassination, ensured that discrimination based on race, colour, religion, sex and national origin would be made illegal. It outlawed racial segregation in schools and public housing and put an end to employment discrimination.

The act was the result of the lengthy – and still ongoing – struggle of African Americans against institutional racism and racial segregation, brought to international attention through the hugely diverse campaigns and protests that formed the civil rights movement.

Lyndon B. Johnson, Kennedy's successor, helped force the act through Congress and the Senate despite attempts by Southern senators to filibuster* the decision. It was the longest ever coordinated filibuster, lasting a staggering sixty days before enough votes were secured to end the debate.

In 1972, Title IX of the Education Amendments was introduced to prevent discrimination based on sex in educational institutions. At the same time, it also sought to plug the gap in Title VI, which banned discrimination in federally funded private and public bodies on the basis of race, colour and national origin but not sex.

Title IX was signed into law by President Richard Nixon and stated that: 'No person in the United States shall, based on sex, be excluded from participation in, be denied the benefits of, or be subjected to discrimination under any

---

* A form of obstruction where members speak for so long on a topic that they force a vote to be delayed.

education program or activity receiving Federal financial assistance.' There is no mention of sport in the original text, and a 1974 amendment from Congressman John Tower that would have excluded sports departments from Title IX's remit was defeated.

However, it is in college sport where the law's impact has been most visible. Put simply, the law meant that schools and colleges had to demonstrate that they were providing proportional opportunities to male and female athletes. School and college sport is a huge business in the US. In 2018, according to the National Collegiate Athletic Association, which runs ninety championships across twenty-four sports in 1,100 institutions, $18.1 billion was spent on college sport. Suddenly, in the mid-1970s, programmes that spent heavily on their men's college American football team, basketball teams or track teams, to name a few, had to find a way to equalise their spending to provide the same opportunities to their women students.

Women's soccer was a big beneficiary. It had an advantage too. In England, men's football was 'the national game', an unmissable part of the cultural landscape. In the US it was more on the periphery, and – in a direct contradiction of the unscientific excuse behind the 1921 ban that argued the game was unsuitable for women's delicate constitutions – in the US it was the relative lack of physicality that made it more acceptable for women to play it.

'Title IX was a wonderful driver,' says the head coach of the University of North Carolina's women's soccer team, Anson Dorrance. 'We went from very few teams, competing. Right now, we have over 1,000 colleges playing women's college soccer, more than the men.' Dorrance is well placed to opine on the benefits of Title IX in women's soccer. The sixty-nine-year-old is one of the most successful American coaches of all time, in any sport. He has won twenty-two Division I titles with UNC – for context, nearest rivals Notre Dame and Stanford have three apiece. Later he would go on to manage the US women's national team between 1986 and 1994.

Can you overstate the importance of Title IX? 'No,' says Dorrance. 'Because what it gave us was volume. You can't understate the value of American collegiate player development.' Expanding on the fundamental importance of the extensive college soccer system, he explains:

A typical US player is very athletic, because we are basically drawing from an enormous player pool. Most European countries don't have the number of players in that age group – between seventeen and twenty-one – that are playing consistently competitively as starters, where they are the margin of victory.

A seventeen, eighteen, nineteen-year-old that ends up joining a Man City, or an Arsenal, or a Chelsea doesn't really get to be the player that's the margin of victory. They get on the field, which makes them very good in possession and their speed of play improves and tactically they get better and better, but they aren't responsible for winning and losing games yet.

What happens in an American college for so many players is the pressure of winning and losing is on them. That is what builds the winning mentality that separates the American player. The Chelseas, the Arsenals, the Man Citys, they all do a good job with elite talent but the pool in England isn't wide and deep.

A huge number of the US women's national team's stars have played under Dorrance. Staggeringly, one-third of the players that have won the World Cup with the US have been coached by him. Five players that competed in France in 2019 are graduates of his. Lucy Bronze, the Best FIFA Women's Player for 2020, attended summer camps with Dorrance in her early teens before playing for one year at UNC, and it was the US coach that would initially point England's scouts in her direction.

England's head of women's technical development, Kay Cossington, has been tasked with revolutionising the pathway for England's female players. Building a player pool on a relative scale to that which is provided by Title IX is not an option; instead Cossington is having to search for alternative ways of doing things:

> *I've spent many years studying our main competitors. The USA obviously being one of them. There's certain things that we just can't compete with. We can't compete with Title IX, which gives equal opportunities and access and facilitation in colleges to boys and girls. We can't do that but what we have to do is create something that's right for England as in our country and our culture.*
>
> *We've spoken to players about what they go to the States for and it's two key things really: the financing of education through full scholarships and the level of competition.*

Providing educational opportunities and a high level of competition are areas where it is possible to make gains on the US system. However, the head start and huge boost that Title IX provided meant that the US became the premier force in women's football almost overnight in the 1970s, and to this day remains a force that is extremely difficult to overcome.

While the effect of the Title IX legislation saw the US undergo a more drastic sea change than would be seen elsewhere at this point, it was by no means alone in seeing a significant boost to the uptake and popularity of the women's game beginning in the 1970s. The game had also begun to take off in Asia, with many Asian countries having experienced their own women's liberation movements starting in the late 1960s.

The Asian Football Confederation Women's Asian Cup launched in 1975 with Hong Kong as the first hosts, while the Chinese Taipei Football Association organised the Chunghua Cup, a triennial tournament played between 1978 and 1987, which invited both club and national teams to take part. At the same time, in 1981, Japan would also host the first of five Mundialito (little World Cup) tournaments.

All these tournaments contributed to the pressure on FIFA and UEFA to formally recognise and embrace the game. In 1986 the Norwegian delegate to the FIFA Congress in Mexico City, Ellen Wille, would challenge the 150 men present to finally do exactly that.

'I'd had to fight to get women's football recognised in Norway,' she remembers in an interview with FIFA. 'I wanted to continue that internationally. So I took to the stage at the FIFA Congress, and pointed out that women's football was mentioned nowhere in any of the documents. I also said it was high time the women had their own World Cup and took part in the Olympic Football Tournament.'

João Havelange, chair of the Congress and the successor of Rous as FIFA president, surprisingly backed the call and voiced his support for women's football. He tasked the then general secretary, Sepp Blatter, with leading on the women's game. For the first time in its history, almost a century after Nettie Honeyball and co. played their first official fixture, women's football looked set to be played on the international stage in an officially sanctioned setting.

Two years after Ellen Wille had laid down the gauntlet at the Mexican congress, FIFA dipped its toe into women's football for the first time and organised an invitational tournament, to be held in Guangdong, China, between 1 and 12 June 1988. Despite Havelange's professed support and the evidence provided by the various unofficial incarnations in preceding years, it was felt that an approved tournament was needed as a feasibility study.

At the governing body's invitation twelve teams from six continents took part in the competition. Sweden, Norway, Netherlands and (as it was then) Czechoslovakia represented UEFA. The Ivory Coast, Brazil and Australia took part on behalf of the Confederation of African Football (CAF), the South American Football Confederation (CONMEBOL) and the Oceania Football Confederation (OFC) respectively. The Confederation of North, Central America and Caribbean Association Football (CONCACAF) sent Canada and the USA, and China, Japan and Thailand represented the AFC.

An impressive 45,000 fans filed into Guangdong's Tianhe Stadium for the opening game between China and Canada, with the hosts winning 2–0. Across the tournament a total of 375,780 fans would show up to watch. Progress remained slow in other aspects, however. Still shackled by the idea that women were not capable of playing a man's game, matches were controversially capped at eighty minutes, and discussions took place over the use of a smaller ball (though that idea was mercifully discarded).

Norway went on to beat Sweden in the final, with a goal from Linda Medalen sealing victory in the fifty-eighth minute in front of 35,000 fans. Buoyed by the success of the trial tournament, FIFA finally set to planning its first official incarnation, to be held in 1991.

However, the governing body was fearful of the impact women's football might have on its carefully crafted World Cup brand. As a result, with confectionery producer Mars, Incorporated lined up as the tournament's sponsor, the first official Women's World Cup was actually handed the snappy title of the 'FIFA World Championship for Women's Football for the M&Ms Cup'. The women's game still had to prove its worth, and the games were still capped at eighty minutes, prompting the memorable retort from US captain April Heinreichs that 'they were afraid our ovaries were going to fall out if we played ninety'.

The 1991 competition would again be held in China, with the country keen to show off its hosting skills ahead of a bid to host the Olympic Games. Organisers ensured stadiums were filled by giving tickets away for free and putting pressure on workers from local factories to attend – 65,000 spectators witnessed China's 4–0 defeat of Norway, while 510,000 would attend across the two-week tournament. Taking part this time were Brazil, China, Denmark, Germany, Italy, Japan, New Zealand, Nigeria, Norway, Sweden, Chinese Taipei and the USA.

The USA, under the tutelage of Anson Dorrance, raced to the final in their maiden tournament. In the deciding game against Norway they emerged 2–1 winners courtesy of a goal in each half from Michelle Akers, who would win the Golden Boot with ten goals. The success of the 1991 competition was hugely significant to the trajectory of the game. Qualifying tournaments meant a more regular schedule of international fixtures, while the seal of approval from the governing body acted as a catalyst for federations to jump on the women's football bandwagon.

The 1991 victory was also a testament to the impact of Title IX on the development of women's football in the country. 'When I was hired in 1986 the United States had never won a game in international competition and five years later we were world champions,' explains Dorrance. 'The way we established the United States is the same way I established my collegiate programme.'

Another key component to the success of the US Women's National Team in 1991 was the system Dorrance adopted. He explains the mentality behind it, saying:

We pressed, even with only three substitutions. I wanted to design a system I personally would hate to play against. The kind of players I hate to play against are the ones that are in my face, challenging me on every fifty–fifty ball, not letting me

*breathe. In 1991 the system we played was 3–4–3. Why? Because
the easiest system to press out of is the 3–4–3.*

*I'm convinced that there are many reasons why we won in
'91. Our mentality was the primary reason, we competed like
there was no tomorrow and we beat teams to death.*

*What was interesting was that almost every team we
played in 1991 played 4–4–2 and we were such a different
team. When we lose the ball, we go get it. If we've lost the ball
next to your corner flag, that's where we're going to hunt it.
We don't draw back and visit the bunker and twiddle our
thumbs. We go out and reach out and try to grab you by the
throat and squeeze the frigging air out of you. So that was our
philosophy.*

Back home, despite the team's success, the impact was
not immediately obvious. Few would see the historic moment
of their victory as the game was not picked up by broadcasters in the US. In fact the players returned to the States
with minimal fanfare – a reception at the White House
with the then president, George Bush, a highlight. Dorrance
remembers a telling encounter:

*While we were flying back from China, Michelle Akers was
sitting next to this old woman and Michelle was all excited
because, of course, she had just won the world championship.
This old woman leaned into her and said: 'What were you
doing in China?' Michelle of course, just so excited, said: 'Well
we went and we played in the first women's world championship
and we're world champions.' The old lady turns to her and says:
'Uh, that's nice, dear.'*

That was the reaction. No one in the United States knew or cared because there wasn't any coverage. The only newspaper that covered us was USA Today. *By the time we got to the semis I think the* Los Angeles Times *and the* New York Times *jumped in, but no one really followed us; we were anonymous.*

However, in subsequent years, the foundation laid by the team in China would prove to be a massively important part of the development of women's football in the USA, as we will see in the next chapter.

Four years later, in 1995, the tournament was finally named the FIFA Women's World Cup and matches were extended to ninety minutes (although FIFA agreed that each team would be allowed to take a two-minute timeout in each half of the game). With Scandinavia at the heart of the growth of the women's game, the second FIFA-sanctioned tournament took place in Sweden.

Many of the teams taking part were familiar, but along with fellow newcomers Australia and Canada, 1995 would also be England's first appearance at an official Women's World Cup. After the FA had lifted the ban in 1970 the WFA formally set up an England women's team the following year, replacing Harry Batt's unofficial team. The WFA-sanctioned outfit played its first official match against Scotland on 18 November 1972, almost one hundred years after the first men's international had been played, winning 3–2, with Sylvia Gore scoring the team's first goal. Under the WFA, England would also compete in the earliest European-wide tournaments organised by UEFA in 1982–84 and 1987, as well as in Euro 1991, where they lost 6–1 to Germany in the quarter-finals and failed to qualify for the 1991 World Cup as a result.

In 1993, partly prompted by the new UK Sports Council policy document on women in sport, which recommended that all separate women's and men's governing bodies merge, and the orders from FIFA that all football should come under one roof, the FA finally turned towards the women's game, taking control of its running from the WFA and its Sports Council grant funding. Former international Julie Hemsley was appointed to the FA Council, as the first female member.

The change wasn't universally welcomed, however, with some concerns voiced about what the takeover meant, in part because it was somewhat thrust upon them, as, according to historian Raf Nicholson: 'in July 1992 the FA proposed to the UK Sports Council that they would take over direct responsibility for the area of development of women's football. Therefore they requested that the sports council should pay the grant aid directly into the FA's own accounts and that the FA would then distribute it to women's football as they saw fit. This duly occurred.'. The former secretary of the WFA until it folded, Linda Whitehead, told the *Independent* that 'a lot of people felt very bitter . . . It wasn't what they wanted to do, it was the way they did it – they just rode roughshod all over us.'

When Kelly Simmons, the current head of the women's professional game for the FA, reflects back on that change of almost thirty years ago, the stand-out issue was the size and scope of the FA at the time. 'It was a very small organisation in those days,' she says. 'It had very little money, it didn't do anything grassroots, it didn't really do anything outside of England, the FA Cup and governance or discipline stuff . . . You have to remember that this was around when pay-to-view TV was only just coming in. There just weren't those big commercial deals. The Premier League was only a year old.

'Culturally, it was a very male organisation,' Simmons continued. 'It was probably an all-male FA council and they didn't have a board then. The FA was 95 per cent men's football but there were definitely pockets of support and some really key male allies that got it going.'

After taking over from the WFA, the governing body tasked Ted Copeland with managing England. Under his leadership the team reached the semi-finals of Euro 1995 (where they again lost to Germany, 6–2 on aggregate over two legs), which meant they secured qualification for the 1995 World Cup.

Coverage of England's debut at the FIFA Women's World Cup was sparse, with highlights shown on TV but minimal newspaper reportage. The *Independent* summed up the mood:

It is a pleasantly sunny afternoon at Bisham Abbey. England's footballers – Alan Shearer, David Platt, that platinum blond – are training for the Umbro Cup under the gaze of the media. Suddenly, one of the television cameramen receives a raucous request: 'We're over here, Amos!' And Amos swings his lens round obligingly to the neighbouring pitch, where a group of women in shorts have gathered around a figure with a microphone.

'You can forget about the Umbro Trophy,' the figure announces, 'because our women's team are off to Sweden to

compete in their first-ever World Cup finals.' But for all that
good-natured rhetoric, the British public's attention is not
remotely likely to follow the same arc as Amos's camera. The
women in question, however, were investing no less effort than
their feted male counterparts to prepare for a tournament that
could earn them unprecedented attention.

England travelled to the tournament without a sponsor, and the twenty-strong squad had just five days of training together prior to their first game. The hosts Sweden, plus Japan and Canada, in contrast, had spent the two months prior to the tournament together in preparation. The defending world champions, the US, had had their jobs secured and wages paid out of a reported budget of $1.25 million to enable them to train together from January. 'We can't compete with that,' said Ted Copeland.

They couldn't. 'England Crash Out' read the small headline in the *Reading Evening Post* after the quarter-final defeat to Germany, 'Despite a Superb Display by Goalkeeper Pauline Cope'. Despite their funding and preparation, the USA wouldn't last much longer, going out following a 1–0 semi-final defeat at the hands of eventual winners Norway.

There were three key takeaways from this second FIFA-backed tournament. Firstly, the very fact that this was the second edition of the competition showed that the world governing body did not intend to pull the rug out from under women's football any time soon and that was critical to the pursuit of domestic backing from federations. Secondly, with the Atlanta Olympics welcoming football into the fold in 1996 and the World Cup serving as qualifying, the seven highest-ranked teams (England were ineligible) were able to join their USA hosts in competing in back-to-back elite competitions. Finally, with Sweden, Norway and Denmark all reaching the quarter-finals and the game developing in Germany the increased strength of women's football in Europe was on full display.

10 – The pioneers

Why was Scandinavia at the forefront of women's football from the 1970s to the early 2000s? What put Denmark, Norway and Sweden ahead of the curve?

The Scandinavian countries (and the other Nordic countries of Iceland and Finland) have long been at the vanguard for gender equality. They were among the first countries in the world to give women the vote and to bring in legislation promoting a more equitable society, such as through preventing the termination of employment due to marriage or parenthood.

Sweden, Norway and Denmark have some of the smallest average gender pay gaps in the world, with 7.6 per cent, 5 per cent and 4.9 per cent respectively. This compares to 16 per cent in the United Kingdom, 18.5 per cent in the US and 15.3 per cent in Germany. The Nordic countries similarly outperform much of the rest of the world in terms of their low rates of gender employment inequality, a metric based on the difference between the share of women and men who are employed or looking for work as a percentage of their respective population.

Building a society around equality and social responsibility in this manner has not only led to the well-known monopoly of the Nordic countries on the top spots of the UN's annual World Happiness Report,* but has also meant that

---

* In 2021, Finland came first, Denmark were in second place, Iceland fourth, Norway fifth and Sweden seventh.

historically these countries have been more conducive to the idea of women and girls playing football than has been the case elsewhere. The right of women to play football was part of a broader movement for equality.

In Norway, women's football was played as early as 1928 – figure skater Sonja Henie, a three-time Olympic champion and Hollywood actress, was the star attraction in one of the early games – while in Sweden from 1918 charity matches were played against men's teams, much like in England.

However, even in such progressive Scandinavian societies the women's game was not universally accepted in its infancy, with its progress requiring the determined efforts of many individuals and groups. One such person who played a key role in advancing the Norwegian women's game was Målfrid Kuvås, dubbed 'the mother of women's football in Norway'. Kuvås began playing in 1952, aged ten, for Børsa Boys' Team in Sør-Trøndelag, where she grew up. She was also a talented skater who took part in athletics and handball in addition to football.

In 1970 Kuvås was instrumental in organising the first women's match in Norway since the exhibition games of the late 1920s, to be played between Amazon Grimstad and her own team, from the multidisciplined sports club BUL, Oslo. More than 5,000 spectators were in attendance to witness Grimstad's Else Vasstøl – known as the 'blonde Pelé' – score twice, before Kuvås's BUL, Oslo team ultimately emerged 4–2 winners.

That game, as with all those played by women's teams at the time, was organised outside of the jurisdiction of the Norwegian FA. Kuvås and her team were instrumental in applying pressure on the governing body to formally recognise women's football, however, which eventually happened in 1976, with the national team founded two years later.

Across the border in Sweden there had been a similar upswing in the popularity of the sport during the 1960s. In 1964 an unofficial international took place between a team from Löberöd, in the south of the country, and a team made up of players from a number of Danish sides, while tournaments for girls were also hosted by youth centres and universities throughout the latter half of the decade, with teams beginning to crop up all across the country.

By the end of the decade various teams across Sweden, unaware of the growth of the game outside their orbit because of a lack of coverage, were making preliminary attempts to establish local leagues. One of the most influential of these pioneering teams was Öxabäcks IF, which was founded in 1966 in a village with a population of around 900. Öxabäcks, which was formed by women textile workers in the Gefa AB factory, would play a critical role in setting up regional and national leagues, in attracting media interest, and in inspiring women to set up other teams such as Malmö, Umeå and Göteborg. They would also be key in pressuring the regional associations and eventually the Swedish FA into backing the women's game. By 1969 Stockholm, Malmö and Gothenburg all had their own leagues. Later that same year, the Swedish government committed to supporting non-elite sport in a drive to boost public health, but the Swedish FA still remained far from convinced that it should open its doors to women's football.

The growth of the game soon became impossible to ignore, however, with the number of licensed women's players increasing from 728 in 1970 to 4,901 in 1971 thanks to the rise of local women's teams and regional leagues. That same year, as the pressure from UEFA and the unofficial World Cups also began to bite, the Swedish Football Federation finally appointed a committee to explore the option of the governing body organising the women's game. Despite the committee having concluded that there were specific risks involved in women playing football from a physiological point of view, the 'very rapid and partially out-of-control development' of the women's game nationally meant that the Swedish Football Federation finally took women's football under its wing in 1972. The following year a women's championship was established, with Öxabäcks going on to win the inaugural competition, and the first formal international match was played. By 1980 there were 26,522 licensed players in the country.

In 1984, eleven years after their first recognised international, Sweden won the Euros, with the team spearheaded by their talismanic striker Pia Sundhage, who would later go on to coach the national side from 2012 to 2018. In all, across eleven European Championships between 1984 and 2013, Sweden won once and finished runners-up three times, while Norway won twice and finished as runners-up four times.

At the same time as women's football was rising to the fore in Scandinavia in the late twentieth century, a similar story was unfolding just across the Baltic Sea in the country that would finish runners-up to Norway in the 1995 World Cup.

Women's football had been banned in West Germany from 1955 to 1970, with the DFB (German FA) president at the time, Peco Bauwens, saying of the unanimous decision: 'We will never seriously consider this matter. It's not a matter for the DFB. If a dozen women get together in some cities and found a football club, that's their business.'

In East Germany women's football was not banned, but was treated as a recreational activity for women rather than a professional sport. Nonetheless, by the end of 1971 – the same year the first league was formed in West Germany – there were 150 women's teams in the East.

International teams for both East and West were founded in the 1980s, with somewhat differing fortunes. The women's team for the German Democratic Republic in the East was founded in 1989. It would be a short-lived affair, however, with their first and only game in May 1990 (a 3–0 defeat by then Czechoslovakia) played just five months before the dissolution of the GDR.

Meanwhile, the West Germany team played its first game in 1982, beating Switzerland 5–1. In 1989 the country would host the precursor to the Women's Euros, the European Competition for Women's Football, and went on to win the tournament by beating Norway 4–1 in the final. This success prompted the setting up of the Women's Bundesliga in 1990.

Former Germany international and head coach Silvia Neid, who was eighteen when asked to take part in that first West German game, said:

Our first international match in 1982 was a milestone for me, of course. Gero Bisanz [the national team's coach] did a fantastic job there. Before he could do anything, he had to work out where he was going to find players, as there wasn't a Women's Bundesliga at that point. There were two training sessions, one in the north of the country and one in the south, each with thirty players. Sixteen of them made it through that process to play in the first international. There was a crowd of 5,000 in Koblenz, but we soon realised that some of them had only come along to make fun of us, which annoyed us. But of course this match was an important starting point, as was playing the Women's DFB Cup final before the men's final in Berlin. I managed to get Goal of the Month there in 1988.

Success was and remains the bottom line. Without success we wouldn't have had the media interest, and without the media interest we wouldn't have had the inflow into the clubs. It was also tremendously important for us as a national team, as we could then say: 'We still need an assistant coach or a physiotherapist.' The conditions just kept improving after that.

Success bred success and then some. Germany won the Euros eight times between 1989 and 2013. After being World Cup runners-up in 1995 they went on to win the tournament in 2003 and 2007, followed by Olympic gold in 2016.

The dominance of the German and Scandinavian international teams during this period was bred at club level. In England today there is increasing recognition of the fact that the skill gap between men's and women's football is down to the lack of professionalism and investment in the development of the women's game. These were conversations that had happened much earlier in Germany and the Nordic countries, where healthy domestic leagues provided training to the most elite players that would help to close that historic gap in development.

Nowhere were the effects of this grassroots approach clearer than in the women's Champions League (or UEFA Women's Cup, as the first eight editions were known) of the early 2000s. Between 2002 and 2015, German teams won nine times: Frankfurt on four occasions, Turbine Potsdam and Wolfsburg twice each, and Duisberg once. Meanwhile, the pioneering Umeå IK, who were Swedish league winners seven times from 2000 to 2008, became the first (and still only) Swedish winners of the Champions League in 2003 and 2004. During this fourteen-year period of German and Swedish dominance of the Champions League, only two other teams got a look-in, both of them pioneers within their own domestic leagues.

In England, between the FA taking control of women's football in 1993 and the launch of the Women's Super League in 2008, one team dominated. Having been founded by Vic Akers in 1987, Arsenal would go on to become the most successful women's team in England, credited with leading the charge to popularise the women's game and pioneering the concept of men's teams' involvement in the women's game during that period. They won twelve titles prior to the first season of the Women's Super League in 2011 (and have won three times since) with Croydon's three titles, Doncaster Belles' two titles and seven second-place finishes, and Everton's solo title and five second-place finishes making them the club's closest rivals during that time.

Akers was critical to the team's success and development. The former left back, who spent his career primarily playing in the Third and Fourth Divisions, joined Arsenal on his retirement to work on the club's community schemes and founded the women's team. He was given the job as kit man to the men's first team under George Graham but made sure he was able to keep his role with the women's side.

'We didn't have a lot of money,' Akers told *The Offside Rule* in 2016. 'We relied on training for a few hours in the evening because the girls worked during the day. Sometimes we wouldn't start until at least 9 p.m. Some of the players had to travel quite a distance but we pushed on with it because their effort was unbelievable. They were so committed and they needed all the help they could get at that time.'

Akers had a brilliant eye for scouting – as is still in evidence today in his work for his former assistant and current Chelsea manager Emma Hayes – and with the backing of the board and former Arsenal vice chairman David Dein he was able to provide jobs for some of his players within the club that took them as close to professionalism as was possible. Under his initiative, Arsenal's women combined playing with admin roles, box office jobs and kit washing. Few women's teams of the time were embraced by their men's parent clubs in this way. Though the support may seem minimal in the context of today's investment, the fact that Arsenal's women were formally recognised by the club, able to pull on the shirt and to use the brand, was hugely significant.

Akers demanded a lot from his players and placed an emphasis on physical fitness and healthy living – likely influenced by the radical changes Arsène Wenger intro-duced in this respect on the men's side.

As a driving force in the development of the women's game in England, Arsenal organised invitational tournaments in the absence of a national league and Akers advocated for more from the FA too, pushing for Women's FA Cup finals at Wembley long before the first final would be played in the national stadium in 2015.

The Gunners would win their first trophy under Akers in 1992 when they lifted the League Cup in the same season they won promotion to the Women's Premier League. The team would win the title the following year to kick-start their domination of women's football in England through the 1990s and 2000s, with the likes of forward Julie Fleeting, goalkeeper Emma Byrne, midfielder Katie Chapman, right back Alex Scott, England top-scorer Kelly Smith, defender Faye White and the forward Rachel Yankey just a small number of the influential players to play under Akers.

The jewel in the crown of the team's dominance was their 2007 victory over Swedish team Umeå to lift the Champions League, then called the UEFA Cup. The final was played over two legs and Alex Scott's injury-time strike in Sweden would give the underdogs a narrow lead going into the home leg at Borehamwood. Umeå boasted Brazil-ian legend Marta and Swedish forward Hanna Ljungberg in their squad but the Gunners dug deep to hold out the potent visiting team in front of 3,467 fans.

Arsenal blazed a trail that would inspire the investments of many English clubs in women's football, including the current ownerships of Chelsea and Manchester City, two clubs that have arguably overtaken the Gunners in recent years in terms of infrastructure and investment.

Meanwhile, across the Channel, a similar story unfolded seventeen years after Akers launched Arsenal's women's team, but in this case the man to have his attention drawn to the women's game was in charge of the purse strings rather than pulling on them.

Olympique Lyonnais's owner-president Jean-Michel Aulas is another that has played a game-changing individual role in the growth of women's football. In 2004, seventeen years after he took ownership of the French side, Aulas decided the club should have a women's team. This decision did not come about due to the type of significant broader growth in the game that would simply make this an advantageous move from a PR point of view. Instead, the decision was motivated by a personal belief in equality, stemming from his upbringing and education, and an almost activist desire for broader social change.

Over a Zoom call at the height of the COVID-19 pandemic in August 2020, shortly after Lyon women had lifted their seventh Champions League title, Aulas explained:

The changes that had to happen when I started in the football domain in 1987 in a sense were the changes that I thought had to happen outside of football. Within football there was a huge resistance to the types of changes I wanted to make, inside clubs, inside the federation and in society in a general sense. I thought I had to take responsibility to proceed with those changes, and for that I needed credibility and also the means to be able to

Nettie Honeyball, thought to be the pseudonym of middle-class Londoner Mary Hutson, was a founder of the British Ladies' Football Club that played in the late 1800s and early 1900s. She launched the side with the aim of challenging views on the role of women in society at the time.

The Dick, Kerr railway and tram plant was converted into a munitions factory during the First World War and would birth one of the most famous women's football teams of the era. At its peak, prior to the ban on women's football from Football Association-affiliated grounds, the team attracted 53,000 fans to Goodison Park for a friendly on Boxing Day in 1920.

Around 850 female machinists at the Ford car plant in Dagenham took strike action for three weeks after they were reclassified as 'unskilled' workers, a move that would have seen them being paid 15 per cent less than their male colleagues.

The Women's Basketball Coaches Association and their supporters protest in support of the Title IX legislation during the two semi-final games of the Women's Final Four.

Sylvia Gore, the scorer of England's first official goal, and teammates Paddy Mcgroarty and Pat Davies train at Wembley ahead of their first official international game against Scotland at Ravenscraig Park, Greenock.

Formed in 1949 by Bolton Wanderers scout and referee Percy Ashley, the Manchester Corinthians were the dominant team playing during the fifties and sixties and frequently competed abroad, including at a tournament in Reims in 1970.

The opening ceremony of the unofficial World Cup held in Mexico, 1970. 110,000 people watched the final between the hosts and Denmark, which the Danes won.

Sir Denis Follows, FA secretary during the 1966 World Cup, would lift the ban on women's football in 1970 as one of his last acts before leaving the organisation.

Michelle Akers (centre) and her teammates Julie Foudy (left) and Carin Jennings-Gabarra (right) celebrate a 2–1 victory over Norway in their final match at the first FIFA-sanctioned World Cup, snappily named the 'FIFA World Championship for Women's Football for the M&Ms Cup', in 1991.

Mia Hamm was described as the 'most marketable soccer player ever' after the United States won a second World Cup in 1999. A whole range of merchandise featuring Hamm's image was produced, including a Barbie and her own computer game, 'Mia Hamm's Soccer Shootout'.

Rachel Yankey, who became England's first professional female footballer when she joined Fulham, takes the ball past Claire Utley of Doncaster Belles during the FA Cup Final at Selhurst Park in May 2002.

Arsenal women won a historic quadruple in 2007, becoming the first English team, and only at the time of writing, to have won a European title.

After Toronto Police Constable Michael Sanguinetti told a university safety forum that 'women should avoid dressing like sluts in order not to be victimised', 'Slutwalk' protests were born in 2011, calling for an end to rape culture. They swept across the world.

Saudi Arabia's Sarah Attar competes in the women's 800m heats at London 2012, as Saudi Arabia, Qatar and Brunei sent women to compete at the Games for the first time.

England women have their own 'Gazza's tears' moment after Laura Bassett's own goal in their semi-final against Japan, which, with extra time looming, sent the team crashing out of the 2015 World Cup.

Brazilian legend Marta makes an impassioned speech on live TV, appealing for girls in Brazil to pick up the baton following her team's exit from the Women's World Cup in 2019.

Olympic gold medallist and two-time World Cup winner Megan Rapinoe gives a speech at the White House to mark Equal Pay Day.

accompany these changes in practice.

I have experienced quite significant success and I've been convinced that developing women's football could be an accelerator to developing the values that I generally share.

Meetings with FIFA and UEFA, as well as Louis Nicollin (the then owner of Montpellier who had championed a women's team at the club), helped encourage Aulas to launch a side, but it was the realisation of his own ability to enact positive change that gave him the most drive. He explains: 'I wanted to try to demonstrate in practice that there were ways to address this problem.'

It is this desire to push things forward, to constantly try to grow and to innovate that has driven the growth of Lyon women. Each hurdle encountered became the next challenge rather than a barrier:

There were quite a few incidents that gave me an understanding of the differences that exist in the treatment of male and female players. One of the departure points was around 2005 or 2006 where I had the opportunity to discuss with the captain of the team at the time, who was also in the national team. I realised that the choice of kits was being imposed on female players, in contrast to the male players who had complete freedom and independence in choosing their own kits.

After this conversation I discussed with the chairman of the France Football Federation at the time to say that this had to change immediately and that it didn't correspond at all to the vision that should prevail about the treatment of women, both in sports clubs but in companies in general.

Then, in 2011, another moment, during the Champions League semi-final against Arsenal in London, brought to light the unacceptable differences in the treatment that existed.

There, at a rain-soaked Borehamwood, Aulas himself had stood in the changing room at half-time wringing out drenched kits for players to put on before the match resumed because they had no change of kit at the break. 'I thought that the best way to address this was to struggle to get comparable and equal treatment between all players regardless of their gender by providing full and equal investment in equipment and in infrastructure and in any practical logistics, and we had the means to make this happen concretely.'

Lyon's star player in recent years, the Norwegian forward Ada Hegerberg, has seen that shift in the club's investment strategy first-hand. Hegerberg points out the immediately obvious impact it has had, saying:

We shouldn't forget that maybe eight years ago the team didn't even have a locker room. Now we are at a point where we're regularly at the same ground as the men – which is in my eyes essential; that should be modern football today: keep the woman's and the men's side in the same facility to create the same atmosphere, to create that culture. There's still things to do at Lyon. That's why it's so important that we keep on pushing.

Aulas maintains close relationships with his players of both teams, which has been another key component to the success of a women's team that won fourteen consecutive league titles before Paris Saint-Germain ended their record-breaking run in 2021. He describes making the time to take the calls of players and to build relationships with them as a 'personal investment', which he tries to maintain not just with the first-team players or home-grown players of both sides but the academy players and international stars too:

> *It is very important for me not because it's absolutely necessary in a general sense, but because it is something that can be very personally enriching, for both sides. It is something I do in all my companies, because it's a win-win situation. A personal connection with and availability to the players helps boost their play. It's very important, especially for high-level players, that if you expect a lot from them then you should also give a lot.*

This has proved fruitful in the women's game and less so in the men's if you measure the success of the strategy in trophies and form. The men have experienced success in Aulas's three-and-a-half decades at the club, and counting, winning seven back-to-back Ligue 1 titles between 2002 and 2008 and having twice reached the semi-finals of the Champions League, but the competition is much fiercer. In the women's game at the time, investments were low and success could be bought and built very quickly. In addition, Aulas's hands-on approach exposed him to the conditions of women footballers in a way that few other owners experienced. Where the majority of big men's clubs either didn't have a women's team, or placed them out of sight and out of mind, Lyon folded the women's team into the arms of the club more generally at the request of the owner.

As a result Lyon became the hunting ground of many of the biggest players in the world, both because success breeds success but also because the players knew they would be treated as professionals, with no lesser standing on the training ground than the men. Maintaining this degree of success is a challenge of which Aulas is all too aware:

It is certainly not easy to stay on top all the time. We have won fourteen French championship titles. But that is linked to a number of factors. One is the quality of the players and the spirit that we have managed to develop within the team, which includes the capacity to question themselves all the time and try to improve themselves on that basis. Secondly, is the fact that we want to invest in women's football at the level required. Even if we already have success we don't want to rest on that, we want to systematically invest. We want to fight not only for titles but also to make female football an absolutely essential and super positive part of the success of the whole club and promote it as a division of the club and not only just as the women's team.

Aulas has managed to grow the women's team from national champions to European champions and into a globally recognised elite side. The next stage is taking the Olympique Lyonnais brand to an even bigger audience. Part of the strategy for doing so is the acquisition of Reign FC (now OL Reign), a team which plays in the National Women's Soccer League in the US. Aulas believes that the purchase of the side adds credibility given the value of US women's football to the sport as a whole, and financial credibility because 'from an economic point of view the US is probably the most important partner beside Japan'. Above all, though, he hopes to use the presence of the OL Group in one of the biggest women's football marketplaces to act as a lever to influence things on a global scale. Just as Akers was able to wield the Arsenal name and the respect he had garnered from his work in the men's game to aid his quest to grow the women's, Jean-Michel Aulas has recognised the hugely significant role he can play as a power broker in the men's game to push the women's. Neither has been motivated purely by financial gain but both recognised the huge potential for profitability for the game and how that can be a driver towards equality of opportunity.

International tournaments have aided this work, acting as catalysts for growth, driving participation numbers and investment, domestically. Success and progress breed success and progress; if clubs and national football associations taste even the possibility of silverware or of a commercially lucrative opportunity they will bite. And with each tournament cycle, the game is pushed a step forward.

11 – Changing with the times

In 2009 the UN under-secretary-general for economic and social affairs, Sha Zukang, voiced concerns about the negative impact on women of the previous year's global financial crisis. These warnings were echoed across the establishment, from the UN to the World Bank. 'Historically, economic recessions have placed a disproportionate burden on women,' Sha's statement read. 'Women are more likely than men to be in vulnerable jobs, to be underemployed or without a job, to lack social protection, and to have limited access to and control over economic and financial resources. Policy responses to the financial crisis must take gender equality perspectives into account to ensure, for example, that women as well as men can benefit from employment creation and investments in social infrastructure.' Years later, in most western economies at least, austerity would do exactly as Sha and others warned: hit women hardest.

The then under-secretary of state for equalities in the UK, Lynne Featherstone, made no effort to mask the truth, stating in a 2011 letter to the Fawcett Society: 'Dealing with the deficit has inevitably led to some difficult decisions which will have an impact on women and their families. However, we are making sure our deficit reduction plans are fair and protect those on the lowest incomes.'

A Labour Party-commissioned report showed that, of the £2.37 billion that the government would claw back through tax credit cuts and caps on public sector pay, 73 per cent would come from the pockets of women.

'Taken individually, the elements that make up the current austerity package will make life more difficult for many women across the UK; added together they spell a tipping point for women's equality,' the Fawcett Society warned of the package put together by the Conservative–Liberal Democrat coalition government. The then Labour leader, Ed Miliband, called it the 'biggest attack on women in a generation'.

Throughout the 2010s ordinary people rose up to fight against crippling cuts, debt and unemployment. In 2010 students across England came together in occupying university campuses, demonstrating and taking strike action to try to stop the spending cuts to education and the lifting of the cap on tuition fees. In 2011 over half a million workers joined a union-organised march against cuts through London. As a majority of the public sector workforce, women were central to that struggle. Emboldened by the new era of fighting back, women were looking for ways to express their frustrations at the economic, political and social systems that had disproportionally let them down.

Helped by the increase in internet access and in particular the rise of social media – between 2010 and 2019 there was a boom which saw the number of people online grow from 2 billion to 4.1 billion – protests and activist movements of women became a key feature of the new decade. They took place across all areas of society and took many different forms.

After Toronto Police Constable Michael Sanguinetti told a university safety forum that 'women should avoid dressing like sluts in order not to be victimised', 'SlutWalk' protests were born in 2011, calling for an end to rape culture. Lady Gaga added her voice to, and thus helped to amplify, the movement against body shaming in 2012 by opening up about her struggles with eating disorders, posting images of herself in her underwear with the caption 'bulimia and anorexia since I was 15' after being criticised for weight gain. In 2011 a campaign of parents and childcare workers was launched to stop the closure of forty Sure Start centres (which provided early years' childcare) in Manchester. Widespread protests were organised in response to proposals by Conservative MP Nadine Dorries that would have required women seeking abortions to have mandatory counselling from allegedly independent organisations, proposed abstinence teaching for thirteen-to-sixteen-year-old girls and put sexual responsibility on the shoulders of young women, not men.

It was against this backdrop that the 2012 Olympics and the 2015 World Cup took place. There was a real momentum building around women's rights and empowerment generally and two such high-profile events as these played a key part both in fuelling that flame and in keeping it alive.

Female athletes would prove central to Team GB's medal table success in 2012, contributing to twenty-five of the sixty-five pieces of bronze, silver and gold collected over the two weeks of the tournament. The historic heptathlon contribution of Jessica Ennis (now Ennis-Hill) on 'super Saturday' was the highlight, but the gold medal haul of athletes such as Vicky Pendleton, Laura Trott (now Kenny) and Katherine Grainger saw many become household names. Boxer Nicola

Adams and Taekwondo's Jade Jones scooped golds as the tournament included women's events in these sports for the first time, meaning both men and women competed across every Olympic sport.

For the first time, Saudi Arabia, Brunei and Qatar sent female athletes to represent them at the Games (though just the two women competitors from Saudi Arabia made it very much a token gesture). Meanwhile, the US was represented by more women than men for the first time in its Olympic history, with female athletes also winning more golds than their male counterparts to add to the country's overall haul of 104 medals. Gymnasts Gabby Douglas and Aly Raisman, swimmer Missy Franklin, tennis superstar Serena Williams and sprinter Allyson Felix were just some of those that picked up multiple golds in London.

It was also a far cry from the Games envisaged by Baron de Coubertin, founder of the modern Olympics in 1896. He had warned that Olympics with women 'would be incorrect, unpractical, uninteresting and unaesthetic', instead relegating women to a place in the stands to cheer on the men. Over a century later, London 2012 would go on to be described as 'the women's Games' by the *Independent*, while the International Olympic Committee said it was a 'historic step towards gender equality'.

This wasn't just a watershed moment for women athletes in general, but a watershed moment for women footballers too. The unexpected euphoria surrounding the 2012 Olympics helped put women's football into the mainstream in the UK. As it was a home games, the home nations pitched together to form Team GB. A skilful 1–0 victory over Brazil in front of 70,000 fans at Wembley, capping an undefeated group stage, helped propel the top domestic women players into the limelight. At the City of Coventry Stadium for the quarter-final against Canada, 28,828 watched as goals from Jonelle Filigno and record all-time international goalscorer (men's and women's) Christine Sinclair for Canada killed the dreams of a semi-final berth.

Instead, the Canadians progressed to set up a thrilling semi-final with the US. Canada would take the lead three times, each goal scored by Sinclair, but the US recovered through two goals from Megan Rapinoe – one of which was direct from a corner – and a third from Abby Wambach, before Alex Morgan delivered the final crushing blow in the 123rd minute, booking the US a place in the final. In the other semi-final a goal each from Yūki Nagasato and Mizuho Sakaguchi saw Japan go through at the expense of France. Canada would go on to collect the bronze medal in a 1–0 defeat of France in Coventry, before two goals from Carli Lloyd handed the US gold in a 2–1 defeat of Japan in front of 80,203 fans at Wembley.

The 2015 World Cup in Canada felt like a continuation of the Olympic success for women's football. The England team exceeded expectations and then some. After losing their opening fixture 1–0 to France, wins against Mexico and Colombia secured England's second-place passage from Group D and into the last sixteen. They battled from a goal behind to win 2–1 against Norway, then stunned a home crowd of 54,027 with two first-half goals to knock out the hosts in the quarter-finals.

And a nation started to believe. The country had taken to the players and their stories: Fara Williams, who spent seven years homeless and hid it from teammates; Fran Kirby, who was struck by depression aged fourteen following the death of her mum; Alex Scott, who had washed the kits of the Arsenal men's first team to be able to afford to play.

They played with heart, desire and an almost simple joy that had become somewhat divorced from the men's national team, where the cult of celebrity ruled supreme. At the 2018 Men's World Cup, England's men's team managed to rebuild a connection with fans and, either consciously or inadvertently, followed a path trod by the women's set-up. The strategy with the men's team prior to the 2018 World Cup had very much been to treat the press with extreme caution, with the players trained in the art of answering questions in a way that inhibited their personalities. In 2018 the strategy changed. Social media was fully embraced as a means of opening a window into previously secretive camps, and players were taken off the leash, allowed to express themselves and their opinions to press and public. The women's team had a head start in this arena. With the game needing press to grow, the FA strategy early on had been to build the profiles of players and to use them to draw people to the game. In 2012 former FA marketing executive Leigh Moore was in charge of that strategy. It was during this period that the Lionesses hashtag was first used, eventually going on to become the team's nickname. Moore told *The Athletic* in 2019:

> We said: 'Let's not rely on others to write the headlines for us, let's write our own headlines.'

This was at a time when scores weren't even being reported, and I felt we had an opportunity where people didn't really know the clubs or the players. Ultimately, people are most drawn to people, and I felt from the word go that our players were going to get the message out there quicker than the clubs.

It sounds strange now but this was at a time when players in the men's game weren't really using social media because clubs were hesitant to give them that freedom, so there was an opportunity for us to fill that gap.

By the time of the 2015 World Cup semi-final against holders Japan there was an air of anticipation. A staggering 2.4 million people tuned in to watch live at midnight on BBC One. In the US, 2.3 million watched on Fox Sport 1, a record for a game not featuring their own team. Meanwhile the other semi-final between the US and Germany drew an average audience of 8.4 million on Fox Sport 1.

With the clock ticking ominously towards extra time at one apiece, Japan streamed forward for one last attack and disaster struck. In an attempt to cut out a cross from the left, Laura Bassett flicked out a toe and diverted the ball up onto the bar. It ricocheted down and just over the line. It was crushing. An inconsolable Bassett, so bright throughout the tournament, buried her heartbroken face in the neck of her shirt as Karen Carney and Claire Rafferty engulfed her. It was the Lionesses' 'Gazza's tears' moment: as her heartbreak was broadcast around the world, the nation mourned with and embraced her.

The often mocked third-place play-off provided a chance for redemption, and a 1–0 defeat of rivals Germany in extra time ensured Mark Sampson's Lionesses returned to a hero's welcome.

The final between the US and Japan offered the US a chance to exorcise the demons of their 2011 final defeat to the same opponent. In front of 53,341 fans at BC Place in Vancouver, with 25.4 million watching on Fox and a further 1.3 million on Spanish-language Telemundo, star forward Carli Lloyd scored three times in the first sixteen minutes to all but kill the game. By that point the US were four goals up, with Lauren Holiday having scored the US's third goal before Lloyd completed her hat-trick. A twenty-seventh minute goal from Yūki Nagasato and an own goal headed in by Julie Ertz gave Japan faint hope of a comeback, but Tobin Heath's strike in the fifty-fourth minute completed the 5–2 goal fest.

The 2015 World Cup was a turning point for women's football in England, the next qualitative leap forward after the popularity of Team GB at the 2012 Olympics. This mixture of full-time and part-time players that had had to graft just for the right to play, the right to own kit, the right to use pitches, the right to quality specialised positional coaching, had exceeded all expectations, and the public had responded emphatically.

The FA took note, and in March 2017 finally addressed the elephant in the room of their past attitudes towards the women's game. With the biggest names in football journalism gathered together at Wembley, alongside a dedicated group who had covered the women's game independently while the mainstream looked the other way, the FA's then chief executive Martin Glenn conceded that the organisation had let down women's football. 'We even banned it in its pomp and we were slow to introduce it [back into the fold once the ban was lifted]. We are addressing these failings,' he said. It was the first serious admission of failure by the governing body.

'I thought it was really important that we said it,' says Baroness Sue Campbell, who was drafted in as head of women's football in a strong statement of intent by the FA at the start of 2016.

We can't go back and change it, but we are trying to do something about it now. That was very genuine from [Martin Glenn]. Without him, the women's game wouldn't be where it is today without any question . . . He was a big part of making this happen and was very supportive. I love being given a challenge like this. I think I should have been a mountaineer or something. I have enjoyed the challenge of trying to put together this great vision for a game that I love, but also that can set a real vision for what women can do in society.

With decades of experience, including as chair of UK Sport during Team GB's record medal haul in 2012, Campbell was handed the power to launch an overarching review of the women's game and work on plans for development.

And the boldness of the plans didn't disappoint. Doubling participation by 2020, doubling fans, and consistent success on the world stage were the headline goals of the Gameplan for Growth. It contained a detailed plan of attack from primary age to elite, designed to bring more people into the game and to keep them engaged as professionals, coaches, volunteers and more.

The plan was all the more impressive given the somewhat bemused reception Campbell received when she addressed the FA Council for the first time:

> I said, 'I have to make a confession before I start,' and you could see all these old boys looking at me thinking: 'Who is this funny woman?' I said, 'I do like football, I've watched it all my life and – you may boo and hiss – but I'm a Manchester United fan, because I grew up in Manchester and I have been since I was a little girl. But I haven't come here because I love football.'
>
> It was good to see them all tutting and looking at each other. I said: 'I've come here because I want to change the lives of girls and women and I believe you own the most powerful brand in sport. If we can't do it with this brand, we probably can't do it. I'm committed to making it happen. If I talk about why I'm doing this, please understand I'm coming at it not because I just want more people to play football. I want more girls to be active. I want more girls to feel they can lead. I want more girls to feel they can be coaches, referees, sit in the boardroom. I want us to use the brand to change what's possible.'
>
> I went and sat down and I could see these old boys all watching me – the execs sit at the back of the room. I watched them all watching me and I thought: 'Well, I don't know what I've done there, if I've shot myself in the foot or not,' but it was true.

I attended that event. It was not just a moment of self-flagellation. The apology was a critical component of the FA's new strategy. Aiming to right the wrongs of nearly a century of neglect is no mean feat. Because those decades of underfunding, lack of support, even active opposition came alongside changes in how women view their bodies, health, exercise, competitive sport, and the further genderising of sport. Attitudes to women in football, sport and in society more generally had not progressed in a straight line.

And yet the potential was huge. As Glenn pointed out: 'There isn't a better rate of return in any area – if you look at it in economic terms – than women's football. Every pound spent on women's football gives the FA a better return than just about any other type of football.'

Half the population had seen their access to the most popular sport in the country massively limited. Only 35 per cent of girls in primary school were given the chance to play football – having been one of two girls that joined in with the boys in my North London primary I was genuinely surprised it was that high.

And despite the barriers, the women that had pushed through against structural and personal odds had proved the game worthy. As we have seen, the success of Team GB reaching the Olympic quarter-finals at London 2012 and of the Lionesses in finishing third in the 2015 Women's World Cup in Canada marked a paradigm shift in attitudes towards the women's game.

Kelly Simmons, who was then football participation and development director, was tasked with talking through how the FA planned to turn the numbers wanted into a reality. She stressed the importance of understanding and overcoming the barriers that prevent girls from playing football – crucially by introducing football in the critical five-to-eight age range 'before they are switched off from sports'.

Simmons and Campbell trotted out the important role football can play in 'fun, fitness, friends and families'. But the rhetoric was backed up by concrete plans. Two hundred 'wildcat clubs' (non-competitive football sessions aimed at introducing girls aged five to eleven to football with an emphasis on fun, football and friends) were rolled out, with plans to expand to 1,000 by 2018. 'Grow the Game' grants were provided to new teams. Ten high-performance centres were planned.

Support for teachers and schools at all levels was promised, with emphasis put on how to make football attractive to head teachers by focusing on how it can complement and boost other areas of the curriculum, as well as mental and physical health.

There were new appointments to drive the plans forward: a head of women's performance, a head of women's coach development, a women's refereeing manager and a head of marketing and commercial for women's football. These were to be embedded within their sectors of the FA and not as a separate women's unit.

The approach seemed more serious than anything that had come before, the proposals comprehensive. There appeared to be a genuine desire to transform women's football and women's relationship with sport generally as a result. But there were also huge hurdles to the success of the project, many beyond the direct control of the FA.

The big question that jumped out was whether schools would bite and where the staff and volunteers would come from. Without active government backing, which seemed unlikely, big elements of the strategy relied on the co-operation of individual head teachers, schools and staff.

Campbell placed emphasis on the importance of selling women's football to schools on their terms, of showing how football can fulfil parts of the curriculum. While this would have undoubtedly worked with the most forward-thinking heads, the grim reality is that the education system, funding and staffing were – and still are – stretched to breaking point.

At the time, the number of schools in deficit had doubled since 2015 according to the National Association of Head Teachers. And school budgets faced real-terms cuts of £3 billion over the following four years according to a National Audit Office report – described by teaching unions as the biggest in a generation.

One devastating effect of the pressures piled on teachers as a result of those cuts was that the suicide rate among pri-mary school teachers in England was shown by the Office for National Statistics to be nearly two times higher than the national average. While 70 per cent of heads were using agency staff and £1.3 billion was being spent on supply teachers as more and more dropped out of the high-stress profession, finding staff willing to commit to such an ambi-tious programme would be tough.

The state of PE was also a barrier to delivery. At the end of 2016 an all-party parliamentary group on a fit and healthy childhood pointed to the 'urgent need to revise the teach-ing of PE, which has not changed since the 1940s, if PE is to play a part in children's wellbeing'. Liberal Democrat peer Floella Benjamin, who sat on the group, said: 'There is no overall strategy for teachers to deliver PE, a subject often sidelined in the curriculum.' But her calls fell on deaf government ears.

Despite these obstacles, it was a good time for the FA to try pushing for influence and funding, as the government seemed to be making good on its promise to use revenue from the tax on sugary drinks introduced in the 2016 budget for school sports. Despite a shortfall in the amount ministers hoped to rake in from soft drink companies, as the firms scaled back sugar content rather than shell out and pay the tax, the government had promised that the £1 billion pledged for the length of this parliament would be found and honoured.

If the FA was in the right place at the right time, catching schools as they looked to use the funding promised, then there was hope. But there were also obstacles to overcome within the game itself.

The importance of having clubs on side in order to avoid the club versus country friction often seen in the men's game was made clear from the off. It was vital that the league's development went hand in hand with the progress of the national team.

But the progress of women's clubs sides was rocky. While clubs such as Manchester City, Chelsea, Liverpool and Arsenal had chosen to plough money and resources into their women's teams, others had struggled. Sunderland had reverted to part-time players, Notts County Ladies had a winding-up petition adjourned and clubs like Watford were struggling financially.

This uneven development meant that a gap was opening at the top of a venture that was still very much in its infancy, one that risked affecting the competitiveness and attractiveness of the league – highlighted by the 10–0 and 7–0 drubbings handed out by Arsenal and Chelsea in the FA Cup fifth round the weekend prior to the strategy launch.

When questioned, Simmons was quick to agree that the funding model wasn't perfect, but a sustainable WSL was a long way off: 'We are investing alongside the clubs. The reality is women's sides are funded by men's professional clubs. With that comes risks. The ideal model would be that clubs are entities in their own right. We're not there yet. I can't see it in the next five years, that's the reality of value and sponsorship.' But she also pointed to the huge strides taken over recent years, resulting in an almost fully professional WSL1.

The struggle to bring clubs on board with the strategy is clear. The lack of a Manchester United senior women's side particularly stuck out, with Glenn, Simmons and Campbell all expressing disappointment that such a global footballing force still didn't have a women's team at the time of the launch.

England's top-scorer, Kelly Smith, also weighed in, saying: 'Man United have maybe been left behind. It's disappointing because they are still a big powerhouse within men's football and for me it doesn't make sense because they have youth programmes but not a women's programme to go to so they are feeding their rivals. At some point they are going to realise that and hopefully set up a team in the future.'

Despite the obstacles ahead, this period in the women's game was marked by a palpable feeling of hope and opportunity for positive change. Promises and plans had been made before. But this seemed more serious, more thought-through, and with backing from such a range of stakeholders you couldn't help but be impressed.

12 – Streets of Oranje

An unfamiliar feeling filled the air as England headed to the Netherlands for the 2017 Women's Euros. For many fans of both the men's and women's teams, this was the first time in living memory that their team, England, entered a major tournament among the favourites. At the heart of this was the togetherness of the team, built through a collective appreciation of what it had taken for each individual to make it in the game.

But England were by no means the only team riding high in the build-up to the tournament. France were ranked third in the world, had not lost in 2017, and had won the SheBelieves Cup that March. Players from Champions League finalists Olympique Lyonnais and Paris Saint-Germain dominated their team, and the country was also gearing up to host the 2019 World Cup.

Germany had dominated the Women's Euros since its inception, lifting the trophy on the previous six occasions. Meanwhile Norway, spearheaded by Champions League winner and 2017 BBC Footballer of the Year Ada Hegerberg, finished runners-up to Germany at Euro 2013. It was very much all to play for.

The hosts themselves were comparative underdogs, ranked twelve in the FIFA world rankings at the start of the tournament. And though women's football in the Netherlands had been showing signs of progress in advance of the competition, few considered them serious contenders. But with a home crowd behind them, and a squad featuring stars from some of Europe's biggest teams – including Arsenal's Daniëlle van de Donk and Vivianne Miedema, and Bayern Munich's Stefanie van der Gragt – expectations still ran high.

Previous editions of the tournament had seen the hosts experience an incredible upsurge both in participation and attendances. Following the announcement of Sweden's successful bid for the 2013 edition, player registration there grew by 33 per cent to 159,305 in the 2012–13 season. This rose to 165,259 following the tournament, and attendances at Sweden's international matches similarly grew by 57 per cent in the 2014–15 season.

While the Netherlands didn't undergo quite so spectacular a transformation following their announcement as hosts in December 2014, the signs were good nonetheless. Player registration increased by 10 per cent in the two-and-a-half seasons after the announcement and, despite a small population, the Netherlands became comfortably the third largest UEFA nation. Their average attendances also more than doubled in three years, and that growth has continued.

The tournament was a marker personally. At the time I sat on the *Guardian* sport production desk as a freelancer doing predominantly layout and a little sub-editing. I had been writing too, but for other outlets. Less than four weeks before the tournament kicked off I was called in to talk about the possibility of writing a regular women's football column for the paper. The brilliant Louise Taylor would be in the Netherlands covering the games, while I would write a weekly column on all things women's football, beginning with the Euros.

It was impossible not to be inspired by the fight of the England Lionesses. I felt close to their journey, and in many respects still do, because as they have risen so has my career as a women's football writer. Few – if any – of the England squad at this point had played professionally for the entirety of their career. But with the Gameplan for Growth launched earlier that year, a future beckoned in which girls would be able to aspire to play professionally from a young age. Their pathway through to the national senior side was now more clearly mapped out by thriving youth teams and there was a bigger pool of talent to pick from as a result.

Against this backdrop, the stage was set for a thrilling tournament – and it certainly didn't disappoint. The Dutch streets were rivers of orange before home games, with every Netherlands match sold out and TV audiences reaching record levels. The hosts belied their lowly ranking with vibrant, skilful attacking football that lit up the competition from the start. Meanwhile, the Lionesses played with grit and verve to emerge unbeaten from their group before an impressive victory against possession-heavy France in the quarter-finals, in which the winning goal was scored by eventual Golden Boot winner, Jodie Taylor.

England and the Netherlands eventually met in the semi-finals, played at FC Twente's stadium on 3 August in front of a crowd of 27,000. For the four million more who tuned into Channel 4 (not including those watching on Eurosport), heartbreak followed as the Lionesses suffered a bruising 3–0 defeat courtesy of goals from Miedema, van de Donk and an unfortunate deflection from Millie Bright in the final minute.

The hosts eventually went on to defeat Denmark 4–2 in a thrilling final that was watched by thirteen million globally. A staggering 5.4 million watched it across all channels showing it in the Netherlands alone (approximately 85 per cent market share). During the tournament, over four million visits were made to the Women's Euros section of the UEFA website. The hashtag #WEuro2017 had over 550,000 social media interactions and over 4.4 million video views. Physical attendances were up from the 2013 record of 216,888 to 240,045. Meanwhile the Netherlands became the first hosts to sell out all their matches – 110,897 people.

The huge disappointment that Mark Sampson's side did not come home clasping silverware, as the highest-ranked side left in play at the penultimate round, was balanced by pride in England's second consecutive semi-final at a major tournament. It was easy to overlook the disappointment because it very much felt like the side was not far off making the crucial final leap to silverware. And of those millions watching, there were undoubtedly girls stepping outside with a ball at their feet for the first time. The effect on girls and boys of seeing women sweat, run, jump and fight should never be underestimated.

While the Lionesses were playing inspirational football in the Netherlands, England won the Women's Cricket World Cup, with former England all-rounder Paul Collingwood tweeting: 'I've been trying for years and today finally my daughters want to play cricket! Thank you @englandcricket women, inspirational #WCWinners.' I did an internal fist pump: it wasn't their dad being a three-time Ashes winner that inspired his daughters to pick up a bat, it was watching the women.

Both tournaments also took place in a year that would be dominated by the global #MeToo movement following the exposure of sexual abuse allegations against Harvey Weinstein. The hashtag synonymous with the movement, started by American civil rights activist Tarana Burke in 2006, was tweeted by actress Alyssa Milano on 15 October and had been used 200,000 times by the end of the day and half a million times by the following day. On Facebook it was shared by 4.7 million people in twelve million posts within the first twenty-four hours. A Fawcett report one year on showed that people who were aware of #MeToo were one-and-a-half times more likely to say that the boundaries of acceptable behaviour had changed in the wake of the movement. The momentum that the pioneering women footballers of 2017 had busted a gut to build was taking place in an increasingly ripe environment for the interest to be capitalised on.

The FA worked hard to try to ensure that the fruits of further tournament success were harvested fully. But there were missed opportunities. It was announced that England would open their 2019 World Cup qualifying campaign at Tranmere Rovers' Prenton Park before heading to Walsall to play Bosnia and Herzegovina and then Colchester United to meet Kazakhstan. With the big men's Premier League stadiums overlooked it was hard not to think that the opportunity to use those games to maintain the Lionesses' profile between major tournaments was being lost. They might not have filled a Premier League ground or Wembley, but not being given the chance to do so and to build a buzz around the games seemed a waste. The attendance figures for those games – 7,047, a sell-out 9,644 and a sell-out 10,026 – were not true litmus tests of the ability of the women to pull a crowd, and Tuesday and Friday-night games did not provide the profile or make logistical sense for fans.

The growth of women's football had been steady but incremental. Attendances had crept up; participation had risen. For the World Cup hosts, Canada, the Euro 2013 hosts, Sweden, the Netherlands and others, hosting a major competition had provided a qualitative boost to women's football in those countries. Watching the effect of the Euros on women's football in the Netherlands left you feeling like a similar qualitative leap is what would be necessary to accelerate the pace of growth and stop these steady steps forward, albeit positive, from becoming expected and routine.

The Lionesses were, and are, overwhelmingly exemplary professionals on and off the pitch. England had one of the best women's leagues in the world backing it up. England employed fifty-one women at senior managerial level or above and had forty-four dedicated England staff working in women's football. The arrival of big-name stars – Heather O'Reilly, Carli Lloyd, Crystal Dunn et al. – from the US showed the progress that WSL teams were making. Six of Holland's title-winning squad plied their trade in England.

Despite all this, England had never hosted a Women's World Cup, and to date still haven't. The FA hosted the 2005 Euros when the competition was a much smaller beast with only eight teams competing. Even then more than 29,000 attended England's group opener at the City of Manchester Stadium and a total of 117,384 attended the fifteen matches in the tournament as a whole. In the twelve intervening years, audiences had grown exponentially. The cumulative audience for Women's Euros matches was 165 million in 2017, up from 116 million in 2013 and forty-eight million in 2009. It was becoming clearer and clearer that the FA needed to bid for a major tournament. They finally did so in August 2018, and later that year England were awarded the 2021 edition of the European showpiece event.

13 – Game-changing tournaments

Nothing can quite prepare you for your first World Cup. Especially when it is being billed as the 'biggest ever' Women's World Cup.

FIFA had a record 206 broadcast-rights holders offering live coverage of every game at the Women's World Cup in France in 2019, including the Friday-night opener between the hosts and South Korea on BBC One. Media interest in the Women's World Cup had never been greater or deeper. The total prize money of $30 million (£24 million) was double that of the 2015 finals in Canada, though still far off the $400 million (£289 million) prize pot for the men's World Cup in 2018.

Perhaps I was too keen when I told my editors that I wanted to cover 'as many games as possible'. It felt like a good idea at the time. In hindsight, it still sort of does. However, in the bubble of travel day, match day, travel day, repeat, it sometimes felt misjudged. Nevertheless, I was hugely fortunate to experience this groundbreaking tournament first hand.

For me, this World Cup began back in 2017. Watching and writing on the European Championship from the sofa I set my sights on France and doing everything possible with my two-year run-up to get there, one way or another. In many ways, the momentum of my writing on women's football reflected and directly resulted from the momentum behind women's football in England. It was an exciting time to be covering the women's game.

The momentum behind women's football was again a reflection of the broader momentum in society generally at the time, with women at the forefront of the battle for equality and of wider struggles. The sixteen-year-old climate activist Greta Thunberg skipped school to camp outside the Swedish parliament demanding action on the climate crisis, sparking a movement of millions. A new blood-drop period emoji launched as campaigns that aimed to challenge the stigma around menstruation gained ground and prompted free period products in schools in Wales and Scotland.

Finland formed a government of five parties, all led by women, with the youngest prime minister in the world in the thirty-four-year-old Sanna Marin. A huge 70 per cent of protesters taking to the streets against corruption in Sudan as part of a movement that would topple dictator Omar al-Bashir were women. The #MeToo campaign continued to make ground, with thousands of women in India walking 10,000 kilometres across twenty-four states to raise aware-ness about rape and sexual violence. Jasmin Paris became the first woman to win the 268-mile Montane Spine Race, while expressing breastmilk for her baby at aid stations. Iranian Sahar Khodayari, known as the #BlueGirl, set herself on fire after she learned she faced six months in prison for dress-ing as a man to watch a live football match. Women were standing up in defence of their right to participate in society equally and these protests and movements were helping to normalise the issues at hand, including women being in-volved in sport.

151

For the England women's national team, the backdrop to the 2019 tournament had been inauspicious. In late 2017 a racism scandal had enveloped the team. Chelsea's Eni Aluko accused the then manager, Mark Sampson, of having made racist comments. Sampson was said to have told Aluko to not bring her Nigerian relatives to a match at Wembley in case they brought Ebola with them, and was alleged to have asked the mixed-raced player Drew Spence how many times she had been arrested. Aluko had highlighted the incidents after being asked to take part in a confidential 'culture review'. Aluko was paid £80,000 in a settlement which included a confidentiality clause but went public on 21 August in the *Guardian*.

Two inquiries, including an independent one conducted by barrister Katharine Newton, cleared Sampson, though both failed to interview Spence or any of the other players present at the meeting in which Sampson was alleged to have made the comment to her. The inquiries also failed to interview Lianne Sanderson, who had been named as a key witness. Aluko would go on to give evidence to the government's Culture, Media and Sport Select Committee, which had summoned senior FA executives to explain the situation.

Sampson was eventually sacked by the FA in September 2017, but not as a result of the racism scandal. Instead, the former manager was removed from his post for 'inappropriate and unacceptable' behaviour with female players during his time as manager of Bristol City – something the FA had known about on his hiring. Indeed, the governing body was forced to pay off their former manager when he brought an unfair dismissal case.

The FA's handling of these controversies was far from perfect, to put it mildly, and so their choice to plump for Phil Neville as the next national team manager – a coach lacking the experience and profile of many of the rumoured candidates, and one who hadn't even applied for the job – drew widespread consternation.

On paper, Neville should never have been given the role. A couple of months assisting his brother Gary's doomed venture at Valencia aside, he had limited professional coaching experience. Sexist tweets that he had made in the past also emerged, drawing fierce condemnation.

Yet somehow, initially at least, the FA's two wrongs seemed to make a right. Neville drew eyes to the women's game from the men's and, as a player, there was no doubt that he knew what an environment of champions looks like. He was emphatic in his apology for his past tweets, saying 'they weren't acceptable then and they aren't acceptable now'. And when challenged over his suitability for the post, specifically regarding his lack of experience working with elite female athletes, he countered that he had grown up with an elite female athlete who had sacrificed a lot to play, in twin sister and head coach of England netball Tracey Neville.

Against the odds, he turned out to be a decent spokesperson for a revived women's game. And on the pitch his team walked his talk. The battling, direct – and, it's important to say, effective – football of the Sampson era was replaced by a possession-based game. Neville's team built from the back and thrived in the system, which better replicated the way they were increasingly playing on a domestic level. It was a team filled with flair players who wanted to have fun and express themselves on the pitch and Neville freed them to do that. But that tidy forward play could only paper over the cracks in the team's defence for so long. Neville also made no secret of his target: returning from France with the 2019 World Cup trophy.

With the eyes of the country, and the world, on the tournament there was a feeling of genuine excitement in the air. Finally millions of people were talking about the football. Not whether women should be playing football, or whether they could, but the games, the movements, the issues.

However, if I was unprepared for my first Women's World Cup, and the effect it would have on me, France was even less so. Steaming into the Gare du Nord on the Eurostar, I was hyped. Paris, though, seemingly wasn't. I bounded off the train keen to join the excited masses; instead there was nothing. No posters, no Women's World Cup presence at all. The Champs-Élysées was lined with Roland-Garros banners. Heading towards the stadium a lone taxi sped past with a female footballer on its side, but with nothing to suggest why. The Parc des Princes itself was low-key, signage nearby reserved for pointing media and VIPs to their various entrances. For all the hype in the build-up, the effort put into the tournament by the Local Organising Committee was underwhelming.

The LOC, though, was bullish. Nearly one million tickets had been sold for the Women's World Cup before the start of the tournament, it said. FIFA's director of marketing services, Jean-François Pathy, said the World Cup had been heavily backed by sponsors and broadcasters. 'Of course we can always do better but I think it's a tremendous improvement from where we've been in the past,' he asserted.

On 7 June, France kicked off the tournament in style in front of 45,261 fans in Paris Saint-Germain's Parc des Princes stadium, with a 4–0 defeat of South Korea in Group A. Two days later England would step out at the Stade de Nice to play Scotland in front of a pretty disappointing 13,188 fans. Phil Neville's team were made to work hard. Goals from Nikita Parris and Ellen White gave them a two-goal first-half cushion, with the Lucy Bronze and Parris axis potent from the off. However, a seventy-ninth-minute strike from Claire Emslie punished their profligacy and led to a nervy end. Drawn in Group D, England had a difficult travel schedule, with games in Nice on the south coast, then Le Havre on the north, before the final group game back in Nice.

As the England press pack departed for Le Havre, I picked up two women's football stalwarts and set off on a 3.5-hour drive to Montpellier for Canada v. Cameroon. It was my first time in a left-hand drive and first time on French roads (bar a brief wedding booze run to Calais in 2016) – and it was eventful. We attempted to record the *Guardian*'s Football Weekly podcast pulled up on a busy road in a village on the outskirts of Nice; I drove for twenty minutes with my door open and an alarm beeping periodically; and finally an exasperating search for the hotel car park around the one-way system from hell saw me drive down a pavement while my companions attempted to carefully placate me in the midst of a sweary meltdown. In Montpellier, Cameroon's chaotic but exciting football caused all kinds of trouble for Canada's resolute defence, though the Canadians managed to hold on for a 1–0 win.

Up next was France v. Norway back at the Stade de Nice, and to say I was a little distracted from the 2–1 victory for the home nation was an understatement. Extreme panic mode set in when I realised I had left my phone on the seat of the taxi I had just leapt out of. With no way of contacting the driver I half ran to the stadium media centre to get connected to WiFi. With the help of Find My iPhone, a French journalist, my fluent dad (from afar) and a super nice cab driver, my phone was delivered to my hotel's reception. The game was equally eventful, with a VAR controversy as Ingrid Engen seemingly got to the ball ahead of Marion Torrent but was nonetheless penalised with a penalty, and an own goal from the usually unerring Wendie Renard.

Back in Le Havre the following day, as we waited for a restaurant table I realised that I had, for the second day in a row, left my phone in a taxi, much to the amusement and mockery of my dinner companions. Again, I was rescued by a generous cab driver who returned it and tried to refuse a tip for the trouble.

England's match against Argentina was an inhospitable affair. The Argentines, determined not to be the group's whipping boys as predicted by many, set out to frustrate the Lionesses, stepping on toes and clattering into players. A goal from Euro 2017 Golden Boot winner Jodie Taylor would be all that separated the two sides at the final whistle.

A very welcome 3 p.m. kick-off in Valenciennes for the Netherlands v. Cameroon, after a smooth three-hour drive east towards the Belgium border, meant a first look at the European champions and their uniformed dancing swarm of fans that weaves its way towards the stadium before every match. Gabrielle Onguéné's strike cancelled out Vivianne Miedema's header to leave the Oranje sweating a little more than planned at half-time. Two second-half goals secured a 3–1 win but the Dutch team's defensive frailties were again on show.

Watching France's final group game, against Nigeria, at Roazhon Park was unlike Nice and Paris because Rennes is much more of a football city. There, the crowd was buoyant, the Rennes ultras occupying their usual spot behind the goal, and chanting, singing and flares were constant. Renard's twice-taken penalty, after the goalkeeper was penalised for stepping off her line before the ball was kicked, ensured France topped Group A, but left Nigeria manager Thomas Dennerby fuming. 'If I gave you honest opinions, they would probably send me home,' he said.

The 2019 Women's World Cup was the first major competition to use the updated Laws of the Games, which included the new goalkeeping rule, and was approved by the International Football Association Board. Yes, Nigerian keeper Chiamaka Nnadozie had stepped off her line, and was booked for it, but Renard hit the post with her first attempt, making the Nigerian's movements inconsequential. The rule would be amended mid-tournament to remove the automatic yellow card as FIFA panicked, seemingly fearing that they would see a raft of goalkeepers sent off in penalty shootouts for unintentional infringement of a rule many were struggling to adhere to. There was widespread criticism over the tournament being used as a guinea pig for the new rules. With VAR used for a major women's international tournament for the first time, despite not being used domestically, there were also concerns that players would not be used to adjusting their game to the new tighter rules.

England beat 2015 runners-up Japan 2–0 in their final group game to progress to the last sixteen undefeated. Two goals from Ellen White secured the victory but Japan – who had taken a young squad to France with an eye on blooding young talent ahead of the 2020 Tokyo Olympics – were poor, uncharacteristically sloppy, and their finishing was awful.

With the group stage complete the team headed north to Valenciennes. England's 3–0 defeat of Cameroon in their first knockout game was a joy to cover purely because it was so utterly bizarre. An elbow to the face of Parris by Yvonne Leuko set the tone for the match. A free kick from inside the box after Augustine Ejangue poked a back pass to goal-keeper Annette Ngo Ndom saw the entire Cameroon squad stand along the goal line, but still concede. Before the end of the first half the team looked as if they were about to walk off, fuming at Ellen White's clearly onside goal being given after a VAR review. Many had not seen anything like it. The team initially refused to restart the match, their manager helpless on the touchline.

After a resurgent second half the Cameroonians were close to another boycott as Ajara Nchout's goal was ruled out for a correct, though extremely marginal, offside. For the underdogs, though, it was another injustice, and the referee struggled to contain their frustrations. With England 3–0 up VAR was again consulted, but ignored, for a Fran Kirby penalty appeal, and the referee inexplicably chose to punish a shove and ankle rake on England captain Steph Houghton with a yellow card instead of the more appropriate red. It is understood that FIFA believed that the referee, whose performance was adjudged as good, made mistakes in her late decisions in the interest of concluding the game with both teams on the pitch – unheard of.

The victory in Valenciennes set the Lionesses up with a quarter-final against Norway. With the excellent Caroline Graham Hansen fit to play, nerves were high. Jill Scott's fourth-minute goal eased them, White's goal doubled the lead and when Bronze's belter flew in for England's third the watching press were on their feet, the frustrations over England's changing media schedule well and truly forgotten. We were riding high on the England wave.

The following day a queue of media snaked around the Parc des Princes for the showpiece of the quarter-finals between hosts France and reigning world champions the US. For someone who enjoys covering the edges of sport, the power of it, the way it is used to influence the world, Megan Rapinoe's two goals in the 2–1 win for the US were delightful. During the tournament a clip went viral in which Rapinoe was asked whether she would go to the White House if the US won the World Cup. 'I'm not going to the fucking White House,' was her unequivocal response.

After Rapinoe's goals powered her team to the semi-finals, Trump challenged her, tweeting: 'Finish the job! We haven't yet........invited Megan or the team, but I am now inviting the TEAM, win or lose. Megan should never disrespect our Country, the White House, or our Flag, especially since so much has been done for her & the team. Be proud of the Flag that you wear. The USA is doing GREAT!'

Post-match there was no sign of Rapinoe holding back

or quelling her views as a result of the spat with Trump. 'Go gays!' said the out-and-proud athlete after the victory in Paris when asked to comment on whether it being Pride month made her contribution more personally significant. 'You can't win a championship without gays on your team – it's never been done before, ever. That's science, right there! I'm motivated by people who like me, who are fighting for the same things. I take more energy from that than from trying to prove anyone wrong. That's draining on yourself. But for me, to be gay and fabulous, during Pride month at the World Cup, is nice.'

The US's defeat of France set up a semi-final with Neville's ambitious England. In the build-up 'hotelgate' broke, when members of staff for the USWNT were spotted looking around England's hotel (they said to prepare for moving in ahead of the final). It was a somewhat trivial and tabloid-style story, but was a reflection of the huge interest in the impending match and a desire to whip up the fans and build the hype around the fixture.

When the teamsheet arrived ahead of the semi-final meeting at the Groupama Stadium in Lyon there were gasps. Rapinoe was benched, later said to be due to injury, while Neville had split up the Bronze/Parris right-wing axis. Where Ellen White's goalscoring heroics had masked the cracks of a shaky defence in England's run to the final four, against the potent US strike force those weaknesses were exposed. The US also won the tactical battle and continued their run of scoring during the first twelve minutes (they had done so six times in their previous five games) when Christen Press caught Bronze out of position and headed in under no pressure at all to open the scoring. It was agonising to watch; there was hope as the in-form White poked in Beth Mead's cross for the leveller, but despair as England's backline buckled when Lindsey Horan sent a cross in for Alex Morgan to head home, and further agony as first White had a second ruled out for the narrowest of offsides and Steph Houghton missed a late penalty. England's dream was over and the US juggernaut continued.

You could argue Neville tinkered a step too far, that the starting XI was wrong, the formation was not up to scratch, the defence was weak, that the confidence became cockiness, but ultimately, while England pushed the Americans hard, the US were a class above.

Perhaps the bar had been set too high. Sue Campbell explained:

One of the things Phil said when he first came in to me was: 'We have a lot of talent, but they don't believe it. They don't believe they're good enough.' [Building up their belief] was a real strategy from him. It wasn't arrogance, it wasn't: 'Oh, we can beat anybody.' He wanted them to believe that they could step onto any field of play and they could win. Winning the SheBelieves Cup was such a big wow moment for him and them. That momentum carried on. I was with them the whole time and they genuinely believed they could do it. This was not bravado, it wasn't big-headedness, it was an inner confidence that said: 'Yes, we can do this.' That's what the Americans have every time they go on the field of play. They do not believe they're going to lose. They can be 2–0 down, and they're sure they're

161

*going to get through. It's in their head, it's their mindset. There's
something in that American mentality from an early age that
says 'we're winners'. He was trying to embed that in them.*

The players were deflated. 'My God, if you'd been there
that night in the hotel, it wasn't pretty,' said Campbell. 'It
was bad. Most of them were still sitting in the courtyard; I
went down at four o'clock to see if they were all right and
they were still sitting there talking. It hurt. It hurt deeply.
I'm not sure we did enough to help them get over it physically or even to some extent mentally. I don't think we realised
the emotional damage it had done. I think it was a long time
before they felt safe enough to put that shirt on again and go
out there with confidence.'

The press was deflated too. But had little time to be. Many
departed for Nice and the third-place play-off the next morning. I travelled into town for the launch of the #FearlessFootball
campaign aimed at eradicating the abuses suffered by women
in football. On the panel was the Afghanistan head coach
Kelly Lindsey, providing the opportunity of an emotional
face-to-face meeting with someone I had worked closely with
from afar over a period of months. With the help of Lindsey,
her assistant coach Haley Carter, one of the founders of the
team, Khalida Popal and a number of other players, we had
exposed the abuses suffered by members of the Afghanistan
women's national team by the president of the Afghanistan
Football Federation Keramuddin Karim.

Later that evening and after a period of reflection on
England's World Cup I was back at the Stade de Lyon for
the second semi-final between Sweden and the Netherlands.

It was dull, really dull, with the great goalkeeping from then unsigned Sari van Veenendaal and Hedvig Lindahl at either end the only saving grace. Jackie Groenen's ninety-ninth-minute goal for the Netherlands ensured a 1–0 win for the European champions in extra time to set up a final with the US.

The morning of the final felt strange. Five weeks' work, not counting the two years of build-up, would be reaching its culmination that evening. Arriving at the ground, this time with a plastic water bottle, having had my metal bottle confiscated previously, my mood switched when that too was taken for not being from the tournament's water sponsor. I may have yelled, 'I'm a journalist not a criminal' at the security team that demanded that I once again ditch it in over thirty-degree heat, much to the amusement of those nearby. Inside, though, attentions returned to the first meeting of a reigning world champion team and a European championship-winning team in the final. It was only ever going to go one way. Rapinoe, returned to the starting line-up, secured the Golden Boot, Golden Ball and World Cup with a second-half penalty to give the US a 1–0 lead after the Netherlands had done what others had failed to do and kept the US at bay for over an hour. A stunner from Rose Lavelle sealed a 2–0 victory.

FIFA president Gianni Infantino entered the field to boos for the trophy presentation before chants of 'equal pay' echoed around the ground, indicating just how effective the American players had been at using their platform to fight for more.

And again there was no sign of them holding back, the

purple-haired Rapinoe saying in her post-match press con-ference: 'We as players, every player at this World Cup, put on the most incredible show that you could ever ask for. We cannot do anything more to impress more, to be better ambassadors, to take on more, to play better or do anything. It's time to take it forward to the next step. A little public shame never hurt anybody, right? I'm down with the boos.'

Despite the low profile of the tournament in France it attracted a global audience of 1.12 billion. Meanwhile the final drew an average live audience of 82.18 million (a 56 per cent increase on the 2015 final) and reached 263.62 million unique viewers. The huge potential of the game to attract viewers, fans, sponsors and more was demonstrated day in, day out for a month. It was hugely significant, then, that the world champions, on the world's biggest stage, stood up and demanded more for the women's game with the spotlight firmly on them.

The 2019 Women's World Cup set the standard for future tournaments. With an Olympic Games the following year, the Euros in England in 2021 and the next World Cup in Australia in 2023 there was real momentum behind inter-national women's football. The COVID-19 pandemic would upend things, pushing back the Olympics and Euros by a year each, putting the Tokyo Games just weeks after the men's Euros in the summer of 2021.

Women's football at the Olympics is a strange beast in that it is bigger than the men's competition at the Games, with senior international teams competing rather than the Under-23 teams (plus two overage players) used for the men's tournament. As in 2012, the UK nations put aside animosities and formed a Team GB side to compete in the women's competition.

Team GB's preparations prior to their arrival in Tokyo were limited. Phil Neville had announced his intention not to stay as England manager beyond the end of his contract in May 2021, despite the postponement of the Olympics and Euros, and the FA subsequently confirmed that Netherlands manager Sarina Wiegman would take up the job after the Tokyo Games. Neville was expected to lead Team GB but days before his unveiling announced he would instead be taking up the head coach role at Inter Miami, the club founded by his former teammate David Beckham. The move left the FA in the lurch and without a head coach for the Olympics just five months before the tournament kicked off. Newly recruited temporary assistant coach Hege Riise, an Olympic gold medallist with Norway in 2000, World Cup winner in 1995 and Euro 1993 winner, stepped into the breach. However, with friendlies cancelled as COVID-19 restrictions impacted travel, Team GB headed to Japan without having played a game since their last outing in 2012. Meanwhile, the US had played twelve times in 2021.

Two wins, a 2–0 victory over debutants Chile and 1–0 defeat of hosts Japan were followed by a tough 1–1 draw with Canada, as Team GB topped their group and secured a place in the quarter-finals. The football was impressive but again goals from Ellen White (who provided three of the team's four group-stage goals) papered over defensive struggles familiar to England fans. Having come from behind to lead Australia 2–1 with one minute to play, Team GB collapsed. An eighty-ninth-minute effort from forward Sam Kerr forced extra time and eighteen-year-old Mary Fowler put Australia 3–2 up before Kerr added another. White scored her third of the game to bring it back to 4–3 but it was too late.

Tournament favourites the US struggled to find their flow after an opening 3–0 defeat to a Sweden team that had eliminated them from the competition in 2016. Playing uncharacteristically conservative football under new manager Vlatko Andonovski the US laboured to second place in their group to set up a rematch of the World Cup final against the Netherlands at the quarter-final stage. With the scores level at 2–2 after extra time the US eventually defeated the Dutch 4–2 on penalties. In their semi-final in Kashima against a Canada team managed by former England assistant manager Bev Priestman, they suffered a shock 1–0 defeat – a first loss to their North American rivals in twenty years.

Canada would go on to defeat Sweden in the final on penalties with the score tied at 1–1 after extra time as Priestman's astute use of her substitutes and tactical nous guided the two-time bronze medallists to gold.

There were many highlights from the tournament outside the surprise triumph of Canada. The Netherlands' record goalscorer, Vivianne Miedema, scored ten times to earn the Golden Boot despite exiting at the quarter-final stage. Debutantes Zambia scored seven times, three in a rough 10–3 loss to the Netherlands and four times in a thrilling draw with China. Meanwhile, Australia looked to be finding their flow under new manager Tony Gustavsson after a period of upheaval. Perhaps most significant, however, was that teams and athletes even made it to Tokyo given the huge toll COVID-19 restrictions had taken on the game and players.

THREE

Changing the Game

14 – Professionalism

The most significant domestic change to come from England's March 2017 Gameplan for Growth was a restructure of tiers one to four of the women's pyramid, announced on 27 September 2017 and due to be implemented the following season.

The Women's Super League was initially launched in 2011 as a summer league as the FA increased its ambitions for the women's game. Teams were made to apply for a place in the new semi-professional top flight (which stipulated that clubs could pay no more than four of its players £20,000 or above) with an initial sixteen teams bidding for the eight places available. The successful sides – Arsenal, Birmingham, Bristol Academy, Chelsea, Doncaster Rovers Belles, Everton, Lincoln Ladies and Liverpool – were handed £70,000 from the FA, with clubs required to match the investment.

After four seasons the WSL2 was added in 2014, and clubs had to reapply for entry into both tiers. Controversially, Doncaster Rovers Belles were relegated into the second division as room was made for the relaunched Manchester City women's team in the WSL1. Steph Houghton, Jill Scott and Karen Bardsley were City's big-name recruits and the team finished fifth in its first professional season but lifted the League Cup after beating Arsenal in the final. In 2016 the league reverted to a winter schedule, with a mini Spring Series played to bridge the gap as the FA looked to align the calendar with the men's season, as well as international and Champions League scheduling.

The Gameplan for Growth restructure switched things up again. The WSL2 was rebranded as the Women's Championship and clubs again had to bid or rebid to enter the top two tiers with the caveat that they could meet the new demands laid out for a fully professional top flight and semi-professional second tier. The new Women's Super League required teams to provide a minimum of sixteen contact hours per week (rising to twenty by the 2020–21 season), an academy, a minimum financial investment and an elite environment, including strength and conditioning coaching, performance preparation and medical welfare. The number of non-English players in match-day squads would also be restricted to encourage home-grown talent. Meanwhile the Women's Championship saw clubs having to commit to eight hours of contact time for players per week, plus matches and a reserve team.

The latest round of applications saw West Ham successfully bid to move from the third tier into the WSL and Brighton and Hove Albion swap the second tier for the top flight too. It also finally helped the FA secure its much coveted crown jewel: the arrival of Manchester United, whose women's team were announced in March 2018 and successfully bid for a place in the 2018–19 Championship season.

After Chelsea and Manchester City had refocused their attentions on women's football in 2012 and 2014 respectively the pressure had built on United, who were then the last Premier League club not to have a women's side. Yet they still held out and the situation seemed to always be 'under review'.

The impasse had not always existed, though. A Manchester United Ladies team that had been created by Manchester United supporters was taken over by the club's community arm in the late 1980s. In 2000 they merged with Manchester Corinthians, a team set up in the 1990s by some of the players from the original Corinthians team of the 1980s. Five years later, after the Glazer takeover, the women's side was deemed 'not part of the core business' and unceremoniously dumped. While this decision was widely thought to have been a financial one, a former employee of the Regional Talent Club, run by the Manchester United Foundation, told the *Guardian* that running the team at a time when women's football was amateur and unmonitored across the board, far from being too costly, was simply too much hassle.

Whatever people thought about United's late arrival to the party, one of the superpowers of world football entering the arena unquestionably boosted the profile of the game. Coupled with the arrival of women's teams from European powerhouses including Juventus and Real Madrid, it showed that women's football had reached a critical point in time where it had to be taken seriously. And it was good business, too. United, until then seen by many as stubborn and out of step, stood to benefit from an enhanced reputation and were faced with being able to expand their extensive sponsorship portfolio into a new market.

Sue Campbell explained the significance of their arrival to me:

It's giving women's football the recognition it deserves.
Recognising that women have a right to play this game, which

is our national game, whether it's for fun, recreation, for competition or for excellence. Raheem Sterling says: 'If you can't see it, you can't be it,' and that's true for women too. If you can't see a player on the pitch, you can't see a woman coaching and you can't see a woman refereeing, how do you know you could ever be it? It's very important. Those big names are a recognition that women's football is starting to forge a really big path for women, and that, I believe, is really important.

I used to go down to my local pub on a fairly regular basis and the old boys in there had seen a couple of things about me joining football and would say: 'What the bloody hell are you doing in football?' and I said: 'Women's football.' Then you'd watch the dialogue shifting and you'd listen to them talking about women's football: 'Did you see that woman, that referee woman, she was really good. Could do with her in the men's game.'

Now those dialogues are going on in homes all over the country, where things like equal opportunities, statutes and policies would never penetrate in a million years. People who are well read and part of the political world understand all those things but many people don't engage with them. If, in somebody's home, in the middle of wherever, they're starting to talk about women playing football, I think that changes mindsets, that changes beliefs. When a little girl comes home and says to her dad: 'I want to be an astronaut,' he no longer says: 'Don't be bloody ridiculous, only men are astronauts.' He says: 'Oh, maybe she could, maybe she could.' If you are having that impact on working families all across this country you'll change the position of women. Maybe I'm dreaming a dream here, but I believe that's possible.

It would not be presumptuous to assume the whole process of the Gameplan for Growth's restructure had been designed to usher in United, in order to have such an impact. They were offered the enticing opportunity to leapfrog into the game's upper tiers, and it looked to have worked. United recruited former England international Casey Stoney to her first head-coach role and signed top players from across the league and Europe. In their first season they would go on to win the league and gain promotion – perhaps unsurprisingly for a fully professional side playing in a semi-professional league.

In their first season in the Super League they finished fourth, and ahead of their second season at the top the club announced the recruitment of US World Cup winners Tobin Heath and Christen Press. The future looked bright, and United led the league until the new year before things started to unravel on and off the pitch. In May 2021, before the team's final game of the season, Stoney resigned, with tensions between manager and club over the training facilities afforded to the women's team during the COVID-19 pandemic central to her departure.

In many ways the story to date of Manchester United's latest dalliance with women's football has highlighted the shaky ground the professional and semi-professional leagues have been built on. Because while professional standards are demanded of players, the reality is that contracts and conditions still fall way short of professionalism for the overwhelming majority of them.

Liverpool lost manager Neil Redfearn after one game, as a lack of support from the club for the women's set-up made the situation untenable. The BBC reported that interim boss Chris Kirkland had bought beds for players as their living conditions were so poor. Vicky Jepson, who stepped up from the academy to manage the side after Kirkland's brief stint, was starved of resources and the team were relegated on the basis of points per game at the end of the 2019–20 season. Meanwhile, the club built a new £50 million state-of-the-art training facility with beach volleyball courts – but no room for the women's team. And Birmingham, who hired Carla Ward as their new manager just two weeks before the start of the 2020–21 season when they had only eight players on their books, were confronted by a letter to the board signed by its players mid-season over a lack of access to the training ground gym, lack of payment for non-contracted players, players earning 'less than minimum wage', poor treatment of injured players and an inadequate squad size.

In some ways the banner of the WSL as a professional league has helped the FA build towards closing these gaps. It has been able to attract a close to £20 million title sponsorship deal from Barclays and a game-changing £8 million-a-season broadcast-rights deal with BBC Sport and Sky Sports that will transform the accessibility and visibility of the women's top flight. All this money coming into the league and clubs will help ensure standards are raised but at the same time, with a number of teams backed financially by wealthy Premier League men's sides, there is also a feeling that more pressure should be placed on them to do more for their women's wings and that too much is being asked of players for too little.

Building a sustainable professional league is not an easy task. In the US the National Women's Soccer League is the third attempt at the creation of a viable professional league. The first attempt came in 2000, when the ground could not have been more fertile. The national team had won a second World Cup just one year prior, this time on home soil, in front of record crowds, including a staggering 90,185 at the final.

The Women's United Soccer Association, founded by twenty USWNT players with American businessman John Hendricks, was the first league in the world to pay all players as professional footballers. The group pulled in initial investments worth a combined $30 million to kick-start the league and the United States Soccer Federation approved the eight-team league in August 2000. The ambition was big, but so was the spending. The league had chewed through its five-year budget by the end of the first season and by the third and final season players had taken wage cuts to try to keep the project alive.

In 2009 the first season of the seven-team Women's Professional Soccer league kicked off. It too would only last three years, but the NWSL would be established soon after by US Soccer. Learning from past missteps, the emphasis was on sustainability, with national team players contracted to and paid by US Soccer as well as their clubs. The NWSL has had ups and downs, with clubs folding or moving, but it has survived eight years and is going from strength to strength. New sponsors and broadcast partners have also helped the league to loosen ties with US Soccer, with the league now run independently of the federation but still in receipt of funding from it.

It is perhaps the repeated failure of viable independent leagues in the US that has led the FA down the path of relying heavily on rich Premier League clubs to prop up women's teams because they can afford to. However, the growing success of the NWSL also shows that independence and sustainability are achievable.

Other countries are also exploring fully professional leagues. In June 2021 the Spanish Higher Sports Council approved the first professional league in Spain. Currently, few teams in the country are professional but from the 2021–22 season the newly branded Liga Ellas will kick off with sixteen pro teams. According to players' union FIFPRO, clubs will be 'legally bound to provide the women players with the same basic conditions as male professional footballers'. For most female players that will lead to a significant improvement of their working conditions. Meanwhile, Mexico have had a professional league since 2017 after men's teams came together with the Mexican Football Federation to discuss the formation of the league.

Little, though, is known publicly of the conditions within so-called professional leagues. FIFA's global report into the professionalism of women's football, based on analysing 282 teams in thirty top-flight leagues during the 2019–20 season, does gives some insight into the gaps that persist compared to the men's game. A lack of medical provisions came up consistently, with the report finding that 26 per cent of clubs did not have a physio, 30 per cent did not have a doctor and only 16 per cent had a sports scientist. Commenting on this, FIFA's chief women's football officer Sarai Bareman said:

*When we're talking about elite-level football, it's important
to have high-quality resources around the players, and in*

particular when it comes to their player welfare and their wellbeing, certainly from a medical perspective.

One of the interesting insights that we've discussed at length already, since we received the data, is that it's the specialist roles within those clubs that really seem to make the difference, in terms of the sporting performance. Those specialist positions, such as nutritionists and psychologists, have a huge impact on the sporting performance of the team.

There are other areas of women's football that have been left behind and are now playing catch-up with the demands of a professional game, with refereeing being the most obvious, grassroots development being another. And, to a certain extent, one can forgive the uneven development because it takes time to build a professional league from the ground up.

However, the protection of players should be, and should always have been, paramount. And when you consider that women are four to six times more likely to suffer an anterior cruciate ligament injury than men, it seems inexplicable that this is still being overlooked.

In September 2019 Crystal Palace forward Gemma Bryan took to social media, exasperated at having been left 'in limbo' by the club after rupturing her ACL in April. A wave of disgruntlement about the neglect of players' welfare ensued. It wasn't until the 2019–20 season that WSL sides were required to provide medical care for their players. In the semi-professional Championship, where Crystal Palace play, that only came into effect from the 2020–21 season and has been partially funded by the FA.

Yet this issue is not a new discovery. In October 2018 Emma Beckett launched a crowdfunding campaign to raise money for three London Bees players, all under the age of twenty-five, two of whom needed surgery on ACL injuries, with one having ruptured an ACL for the third time. During the crowdfunding campaign a fourth Bees player was added to the list of beneficiaries having also torn her ACL. The story is not uncommon. In 2020 Bristol City's Abi Harrison, Brighton's Ellie Brazil and Laura Rafferty, the England and Manchester City defender Aoife Mannion, Tottenham's Jessica Naz, Crystal Palace's Ashlee Hincks, Birmingham's Heidi Logan and, for the second time, Arsenal's Danielle Carter were all sidelined with ACL injuries.

While investment has gone into building the game, those actually responsible for the product on the pitch that clubs and the FA are selling to broadcasters and sponsors have been woefully unprotected, for years forced either to raise thousands of pounds to cover private treatment or to spend months on NHS waiting lists.

In addition the standard contracts issued by the FA often did more to protect clubs from their injured players than to help players forced from the field. In 2018, the Danish newspaper *Politiken*, as part of the Football Leaks releases, showed that a clause in player contracts permits WSL clubs to offload players if an injury or illness sidelines them for more than three months, provided they give three months' notice.

Where male footballers are afforded much greater protections should they suffer one of the most serious injuries that can be picked up on a pitch, with a lengthy recovery period that many say has a big impact on their mental health, a huge number of women footballers have little to no protection.

At the time it was made clear that, while it was unlikely that any of the larger WSL clubs would contemplate invoking the clause, it existed to protect less financially insulated teams. An FA spokesperson said:

> *The Women's Football Contract was designed and structured to meet the unique demands of the women's football pyramid. It was developed in consultation between The FA, the Clubs and the PFA to shape a player contract that the women's football pyramid could financially sustain and one that reflects the recently emerging status of women's professional football in England.*
>
> *It differs from men's professional football, which is more established and better suited to accommodate the additional financial liability of long-term injuries to players. Medical standards are constantly improving and are under regular review to meet the future requirements of the women's game. Any changes to the Women's Football Contract will be made in collaboration between The FA, the Clubs and the PFA.*

Except surely there is an argument to say that, if a club cannot support even the most basic of insurance policies for its players, then its viability as a functioning and sustainable club in a professional or semi-professional league should be more thoroughly questioned.

In 2020 I spoke to former England international Claire Rafferty for the *Guardian* about her journey through three ACL injuries and she told me of the devastating impact.

'You start to blame yourself,' she said. 'I definitely did. I would go through different phases of feeling sorry for myself. Why? Why is it me? Am I doing something wrong? Am I not training hard enough? When actually it's stuff that you can't really see.'

Yet most employers, even the smallest, will have insurance policies that cover workplace injury and, in the case of footballers, it is an industry where the risk of injury is high. Player welfare should not be a choice or an afterthought.

All of this goes to show that the path to professionalism is not a straight one. There will be steps backwards and there will be flaws in the process in every country that attempts to build a viable professional league. However, there is enough global interest and collective support – from sponsors, players, the public, governing bodies and more – to sustain professional women's football and to smooth the pathway towards it. The WSL and NWSL in particular are leading the modern charge and vying with each other for the title of the 'best league in the world' – competitiveness that will only drive further growth. And, just as the early incarnations of professional football in the US provided the necessary lessons for the NWSL to thrive today, so too can each new professional league become part of the larger global blueprint for others to learn from.

15 – The tinkerman

Despite overarching good intentions, the seemingly haphazard nature of the FA's decision-making and implementation of its strategies for women's football over the years has repeatedly split the room. Soaring attendances and viewing figures for international games were not filtering down to the leagues. As a result the WSL went from a single semi-professional eight-club league to two leagues of eight and ten teams (WSL1 and WSL2) to a fully professional top flight and semi-professional second tier in the space of seven short years. Coupled with indecisiveness over a winter/summer league format and the headlong race towards professionalism at any cost, it isn't hard to see why the FA has been accused of being the 'tinkerman' of women's football.

These constant changes did not allow for clubs to plan or set targets for the long term because the goalposts kept getting moved. Often the time frame between each change was not long enough to draw up a proper balance sheet of the successes and failures of the previous incarnations of the leagues. There was no time to fully gauge the effects of the 2017–18 switch to a winter league – which pitted women's matches against men's and in less favourable weather, with a corresponding impact on attendances – before the next variable was tweaked.

The reasoning behind the seasonal switch was clear enough, in fairness. Kelly Simmons explains:

We had to connect the pyramid. Promotion-relegation is just one of those core principles of football in this country.

The reason I thought it would have to go winter was that there were a whole raft of challenges in the grassroots game about playing across the summer with pitches and grounds not open and people playing cricket and all that stuff, but the fundamental thing for me was that FIFA and UEFA have ultimately set your framework with the international calendars; they give you your structure and then you slot in.

Three seasons out of four with a summer league you broke for a major tournament. Then most of those grounds were third party, where they would need to break for five weeks to reseed the pitch.

Despite the logic, the constant change meant clubs struggled for continuity and began to suffer. Notts County Ladies was wound up on the eve of the 2016 Spring Series because the club was not willing to support it any longer. In 2017 Sunderland reverted to part-time status and subsequently fell out of the top flight, choosing not to bid for a licence for the new professional WSL. The shifting sands of the FA's decision-making were not solely to blame for these scenarios, but both demonstrated the precarious existence of women's teams that are heavily reliant on men's clubs, and the suddenness with which a single change in fortunes can mean their continued existence is no longer tenable.

In 2018 the deadline for WSL clubs to apply to stay in the top two tiers closed less than fifty days after the controversial restructure to a professional top flight and semi-professional Championship was announced, with clubs required to submit details of how they would meet the strict new criteria set out by the FA.

The timing was poor. This would be a huge financial undertaking and one that clubs had to make workable within a year. Already very beholden to the philanthropy of men's clubs, the success of the plan was reliant on their increased commitment. Those without the full backing of their male parent club or big investment from elsewhere would likely fall by the wayside.

The effect was damaging. WSL2 club Watford announced they would not be applying to remain in the new semi-professional league, instead choosing to drop down into the amateur Women's Premier League. Two days later the WSL1 side Sunderland revealed they too would not meet the deadline to submit an application and instead said they would choose to launch a 'joint bid' (presumably with the nearby WSL2 side Durham or in partnership with a university) for the top flight in March alongside applications from the lower leagues.

Then Yeovil, vocal opponents of the changes who had fought their way into WSL1 on a shoestring, announced they had submitted an application to stay in the top flight following weeks of campaigning, including crowdfunding to claw their way towards the £350,000 they believed they needed to maintain full-time WSL status, on top of the £120,000 subsidy from the FA.

'YTFC [are] the only EFL or Premier League outfit to host all their female counterparts' FAWSL 1 league games in the club's main stadium,' they stated proudly in a statement which detailed their dismay at the FA plans.

'We have the structure, facilities and ambition to become a full-time professional club given time but we currently do not have the financial support to do this,' it said. 'We do not have the budget to allow our players and coaches to become full-time athletes, unless further investment comes our way soon.'

At the first hurdle, clubs were falling by the wayside – just as voices from across women's football had warned would be the case from the outset. Tony Farmer, who had founded Chelsea Ladies in 1991, said of the decision: 'A year ago Yeovil were WSL2 Club of the Year and applauded by the FA; a year later the FA are writing criteria that could rule them out of the league they won promotion to – it's wrong. Promotion and relegation should be decided on the pitch not changes.'

Farmer launched a petition against the restructure in which he, having started the group FA WSL Fans United, posed nineteen questions to the FA, which elicited a written response from Katie Brazier, head of women's leagues and competitions. However, Farmer was critical of the reply, contrasting a boast from Brazier of the hugely speedy development of women's football since 2013 with the collapse of Notts County to illustrate how fragile the growth actually was.

Brazier also drew a funding comparison with the Netherlands in her response, saying: 'Many other national associations have chosen not to invest in developing a strong domestic league (for example Holland) and this has resulted in their players playing overseas.' But Farmer described that as 'bizarre', saying: 'I'm pretty sure they won Euro 2017.' Many were also riled by Brazier's statement that 'the FA could, in theory, have chosen to withdraw its support to the top tiers of the domestic game at that point [the end of the 2017–18 season when the WSL licences expire].'

A belief in the future professionalism of women's football united all, but it was the speed with which these changes had been executed, leaving some clubs behind despite their best efforts, that had sown the biggest seeds of discontent.

Nonetheless, there was a strong case to be made for the FA's plans. Very few would have disagreed with the proposals if they made a clear attempt to limit the extent of the casualties by coming with a longer time frame, a staggered approach and a more coherent and inclusive strategy for the bottom of the pyramid as well as the top. Women's football clubs, players and fans wanted professionalism. Yet somehow the FA had managed to make them not want it. Sue Campbell, though, believes that time was of the essence and that casualties would have been par for the course regardless:

I remember very vividly a meeting in St George's Park, with Katie Brazier, when we had told the clubs we were going to open up licensing and that tier one would be full time and tier two would be part time. We'd laid out what we thought that meant and that we were going to do it that year. In the room was Sunderland, Donny Belles, people who had given a lifetime to this game. I remember the people at Donny Belles had given me a fair amount of stick. I said to them: 'If I was sitting where you are I'd be saying exactly the same to me, but my job is to move this game forward. I don't want there to be casualties but the reality is that not everybody is going to make this journey. That's a terribly hard thing to say. I don't say it without some regret inside my heart, but I've got to do what's right for the game.'

It's: Do I feel bad about it? Yes. But was it the right thing to do? Yes, I'm afraid it was and I'm sure the people at Donny Belles have a little effigy of me somewhere and stick pins in it on a regular basis, and I don't blame them, but I had no alternative. I had to grow the game and I had to move the game to a full-time professional game. They all wanted to wait another year and I said: 'No, I can't. The longer I wait, the further behind we'll fall. I've got to take the step now.' It was brutal for some of them, I know it was, but it was the right decision for the game.

Right or wrong, there was and is a need to do better by teams that feel they have been left to rot. Campbell says that care of the middle of the women's football pyramid is next on the list:

A big ask for us now is making sure that the gaps don't grow so big that that transition between leagues is almost impossible. David Faulkner [head of women's performance] has put together a new strategy called Closing the Gap, which is about reducing the gap between the Championship and the Super League. He's looking at how he supports the Championship clubs in every facet, whether it's mental health or physical conditioning; we're looking at how we get them to a point where if they transition up they can stay up.

The FA has also set up a new board for the Women's National League as part of a desire to make sure they can get more investment, more support and more education into tiers three and four. 'We've got to make that pyramid really work,' says Campbell. 'I don't want a closed league at the top; it removes that sporting integrity.'

Kelly Simmons is similarly sympathetic to the plight of those clubs left behind. That aspect of the restructure was 'really difficult', she says. But as with Campbell, she considers the casualties of the change a necessary evil in the drive towards professionalism:

> *Without some minimum standards it's always going to be very hard to promote and develop and commercialise the WSL. You can't sell a broadcast contract if you haven't got grounds with broadcast facilities. You can't do a commercial deal if you haven't got a workforce in the club that can deliver those rights. You go on and on and at some point you've got to lock down and say: 'We want to be on TV. We want to grow our attendances, so we need marketing staff in there. We need the right grounds to be broadcast-ready, et cetera, et cetera.'*
>
> *If you don't lock them in, you can't move forward. The casualties are really, really painful but unfortunately setting those new standards was the way to deliver professional football and grow the quality of the product to ultimately become sustainable because nobody's going to come along with all of the money and say: 'Job done.' It's a build project, so we had to lock in raising standards.*

The strategy of encouraging men's clubs operating in the lower tiers of the women's game (or not at all in Manchester United's case) to leap in at the top by meeting the new requirements was undoubtedly effective. The problem was that those who had fought hard to build and grow the game felt they had been left behind in favour of those with shorter women's football histories, but with deeper pockets.

At each stage of the restructure process this has proven to be the case. In 2014, as mentioned earlier, the revamped Manchester City were controversially given a top-tier licence at the expense of Doncaster Rovers Belles, who were demoted into the second tier. Today, no one could doubt the commitment of City to women's football, even if their ongoing investment forms part of the broader vanity and prestige project of Abu Dhabi. At the time, though, the relegation of Donny Belles, until then the only team to have been continuously in the top flight since a national league was set up in 1991, was decried by Arsenal founder and manager Vic Akers:

Donny have the support of all the league's current clubs. I've spoken to all seven and we all feel what the FA has done is unjust – in my opinion it's morally scandalous.

When they made their announcement, Donny had played only one match of the season. To relegate them after ninety minutes is a joke – it's kicking them out. If you're talking about relegation then you should also talk about promotion, and Manchester City didn't win the Premier League [then the second tier], they finished fourth.

Sunderland won it for the third year in a row and yet they'll be in the WSL's second division next year. It seems to me it's more about money than football.

Doncaster's manager at the time, John Buckley, said: 'How do you think I felt telling them that? How did they react? How do you think they reacted? I cannot understand why Doncaster have not been able to throw their hat in the ring and compete for a place. If we finish bottom, then we hold our hands up and we admit we are not good enough. We have never lost the right to play in this division and that is what really sticks in your throat. We may just have to take it on the chin.'

After the removal of Donny Belles, the restructure to open the door to Manchester United and other Premier League clubs with a women's team playing lower down was far from surprising. United's decision to join the Championship instead of the WSL in that sense was shrewd as they could earn the right to play in the top flight from their boosted start. They faced criticism, but with lots of teams shifting up and down it was a more watered-down move than the straight swap of City for Belles.

Also winning licences to join the Championship alongside United were Charlton, Leicester, Sheffield United and Lewes. Overlooked for a place in the new second tier were Southampton, Crystal Palace and Derby County, who were all unsuccessful in their bids to join the division with only twelve spots available for the fifteen sides that bid (including seven that bid to stay in the league).

At the top end there was less of a scramble, with fewer teams able to commit to the full-time demands of the league than the FA had hoped. Outside the existing teams in the top two divisions, the only newcomers to the WSL were West Ham, who had previously been playing in the third tier.

Meanwhile Brighton, who had finished second in tier two, were promoted after meeting the licence criteria to jump up. The lack of clubs able to meet the criteria meant the league, which had space for fourteen teams, launched with an uneven eleven sides, while the Championship kicked off with twelve teams.

In the three seasons since the reshuffle there has been relative calm in terms of the structure. Now the FA has turned its attentions to tightening up weaker areas of the licence criteria, as well as to the support around the leagues, broadcast rights, sponsorship deals and governance structures of the leagues. There are still holes. The salary cap is ineffectual, given teams can provide housing and other non-salaried bonuses to cut across it. As was discussed in the previous chapter, player contracts need work. Critically, though, we have started to see the benefits of a few seasons of overall consistency. Now the FA needs to focus on their pledge to bolster the amateur leagues and ensure the gap between the semi-professional Championship and third tier does not become an insurmountable hurdle.

16 – The best

George Best, Pelé, Maradona, Johan Cruyff, Ronaldo, Ronaldinho, Roberto Carlos, Bobby Moore, Lionel Messi. The list of key players in the men's game revolves around those that shone on the pitch, whether as leaders, artists, creators or grafters. The same exercise in women's football elicits a different kind of list. Yes, the best players are there. But so too are the individuals that pioneered the existence and growth of the game, many of whom we have already encountered in these pages. In addition there are those that have come to represent a snapshot of time, sometimes almost by accident.

The Dick, Kerr Ladies star Lily Parr is one of those. In the 1920s Parr was as close to being a household name as could be, known for a vicious left foot and remarkable goalscoring record. She has become Dick, Kerr's best-known figurehead, but she was far from their only star, as club historian Gail Newsham explains:

She was a great player, and she played longer than everybody else, which makes her stand out more because she was able to amass 986 goals or whatever it was. But there were just as good players as Lily. Florrie Redford, for example, in 1921 scored 170 goals; Lily scored 108. Jennie Harris was another great player.

I think it is my fault in some respects. Because when I first started this journey, when nobody was really interested in women's football, I focused on two people that stood out to me at that time and that was Lily Parr and Joan Morley.

When I wrote my book nobody knew the team's story, it had never been told, nobody knew who these women were. I was working closely with the National Football Museum when it was in Preston and they asked me to nominate somebody for the Hall of Fame and I said Lily Parr because they wanted a historical figure. And that's it, she was inducted into the Hall of Fame.

Newsham describes it as frustrating to see Parr now used as a poster girl for the Dick, Kerr Ladies and women's football as a whole in the 1920s. However, in many respects Parr's elevation is helpful. People often engage with the past through the stories of individuals, of stories they can relate to. As a star of the side that dominated women's football for decades, Parr's face and name act as a gateway into the story of a team, players and a sporting era that is new to so many people. Tell someone that a women's factory team from Preston won 759 of the 833 games they played between 1917 and 1965, according to Newsham's extensive research, and defied the ban on women's football, and it is undoubtedly impressive. But relay the story of Parr breaking the arm of a male player who challenged her on the strength of her shot, or who broke into the team as a fifteen-year-old and scored a hat-trick on her debut, and suddenly the story comes to life and the players become tangible, more than numbers and statistics.

It is also far from unique for a figurehead to emerge to represent a movement or time period. Many may have had qualities or abilities matched or bettered by their peers but have, for numerous reasons, found themselves thrust into an ambassadorial role within the women's game.

One such figure from the 1970s is Sylvia Gore, who scored the first goal for the England women's national team following the lifting of the ban, in a 3–2 win over Scotland in Greenock in 1972. Gore had joined the dominant Manchester Corinthians aged twelve after she impressed during a trial, and would go on to become known as the Denis Law of women's football due to her prolific goal-scoring, having once scored 134 goals in a single season. She played until she was forced to retire with a back injury at thirty-five, afterwards becoming an integral part in grow-ing the women's game as a coach, as the first female director of the Liverpool County FA, as part of the WFA and then sitting on the women's committee when the FA took con-trol in 1993 and was a proud ambassador of the relaunched Manchester City women's team until her death in 2016.

The 1999 World Cup-winning US women's side had a game-changing effect on women's football in the US, making it nigh-on impossible to pick out a single star. And yet Mia Hamm became the poster woman for this stellar squad, widely described as being the 'most marketable soccer player ever'. What made her more marketable than the rest? Than Brandi Chastain, whose celebration in her bra after scoring the game-winning penalty against China in '99 is recognised as one of the most iconic sporting images of all time? Or Michelle Akers, who scored ten goals at the 1991 World Cup and was named alongside Hamm on Pelé's FIFA-commissioned list of the 125 greatest living soccer players?

Hamm's insatiable drive and competitiveness certainly played a part. Anson Dorrance, who coached her both for the University of North Carolina and the national side, described her as 'a warrior of a woman and the culture of the time was that as a girl or a young woman you weren't really allowed to compete and be competitive'. He continued:

> It's almost like they've been raised not to be competitive. The biggest challenge, honestly, when you go from coaching men to coaching women is that the way we raise our girls and young women is to not be competitive, and obviously that puts them at a severe disadvantage in a contact sport like ours.
>
> What I had to do within my own culture was to correct that dynamic but also protect the competitive women and basically point to them and say: 'You know what? That's how we're going to train. We're going to train like there's no frigging tomorrow. We're going to train like we're sharks with blood in the water and that's the way we're going to go after each other. And you know what? At the end of practice, we're still going to be friends because this is what we've embraced within our culture.'

Competitiveness unleashed and embraced, Hamm would score 158 international goals, win four NCAA championships with UNC and two Olympic gold medals, all of which powered her marketability. She had deals with Nike, Dreyer's Ice Cream, Pepsi, Fleet Bank, Earthgrains, Nabisco and PowerBar, appeared on a Wheaties box after the 1999 World Cup and co-starred in a Gatorade advert with Michael Jordan. She was the first modern superstar of the women's game.

There are a number of players that were so naturally gifted they were able to win supporters and drop jaws despite playing at a time when the game was mostly amateur. One of those is Brazilian legend Marta and another is England striker Kelly Smith.

When Smith retired in 2017 it hit me in the gut. Not because it was unexpected – at thirty-eight she had had a career longer than many and had already been involved in coaching – but because it felt like the end of an era. Smith was the player that kept my attentions on Arsenal women growing up. The Hertfordshire-born Arsenal fan had played on boys' teams until she was seven when, as top-scorer, she was kicked out after parents complained about having a girl on the team – presumably showing up their sons.

Her dad started a local girls' team to give her a place to play until she joined Wembley Ladies, where she attracted the attention of the Gunners. Skill, power and attitude oozed from her. She was a cut above the rest. Her stylish play helped Arsenal to the title in 1996–97 and while it was sad to see her depart, for any young woman it was an inspiration to see a female footballer fight for the career afforded to men by leaving for the professionalism provided by the United States – twice.

It also felt like that could only be Kelly. Because going to compete in the Title IX-bolstered US league required someone who could show why women's football deserved attention in England, and that women's participation in sport should be able to be more than just a hobby. And Kelly did more than that.

She would have three spells at Arsenal sandwiching stints with various pro teams in the US and would win the historic quadruple with the Gunners in the 2006–07 season. Over the years she was compared to many legends of the men's game. Zinedine Zidane for attitude and close control, or Pelé, Marco van Basten and Diego Maradona for her flair and striking instinct. For me, Kelly was like watching Thierry Henry at his potent best. But if anything, her impact on women's football means more than the contributions of those stars. Because Smith showed that women's football could be skilful, beautiful and was worth investing in. She showed that women have a right to embark on a career in sport.

If Smith is the most naturally talented player that England has ever produced then Marta is probably the world's most naturally talented player of all time. Pelé himself nicknamed her 'Pelé in a skirt' but she has also been compared to other Brazilian greats such as Ronaldinho and Romario.

Born into poverty in Dois Riachos, a small town in the north-east of Brazil, Marta grew up playing street football with the boys, using makeshift balls made out of plastic bags. It was there that she would begin to hone the silky close control and mazy dribbling runs that became so synonymous with her game.

After a coach noted her skills at the age of fourteen, she made the 1,000-mile trip to try out for and then join Vasco da Gama. Her first World Cup appearance came in 2003 aged seventeen, like Pelé. Brazil reached the quarter-finals and Marta was the star. She was subsequently snapped up by Swedish side Umeå IK and became the first Brazilian woman to play professionally in Europe. She won four back-to-back titles with Umeå as well as the Swedish Cup and the Champions League. Since, she has bounced between Sweden, the US and Brazil and currently plays for Orlando Pride.

Marta has scored in five different World Cups and has been named the FIFA World Player of the Year a record six times. Like Smith, Marta's play elevated perceptions of the game. After Brazil exited the 2019 World Cup following a 2–1 loss to France in the last sixteen, the forward launched into an impassioned speech, urging young players in Brazil to fight to take her place:

Women's football depends on you to survive. Think about it; value it more.

We're asking for support; you have to cry at the beginning and smile at the end.

It's about wanting more; it's about training more, it's about looking after yourself more, it's about being ready to play ninety minutes and then thirty minutes more.

So that's why I am asking the girls. There's not going to be a Formiga forever. There's not going to be a Marta forever. There's not going to be a Cristiane.

Back in the UK, Rachel Yankey may not be quite as big a name as Smith or Marta but she is known to thousands of kids in England as the host of CBeebies show *Footy Pups*. It is hard to overstate the importance of seeing a black female football coach hosting a football show aimed at primary-aged kids on mainstream TV.

A winger with a delicious left foot, Yankey is often cited by England players as a huge influence. Capped 129 times by England, across her career with Arsenal and Fulham she has won nine league titles, eleven FA Cups and the Champions League. When she joined Fulham after a spell in Canada she became England's first professional footballer, with Fulham owner Mohamed Al-Fayed having been inspired to invest in the women's team by the 1999 World Cup and the huge success of the USWNT.

Today, with the help of social media and the general growth in the popularity of the women's game, we are starting to see women players achieve global superstar status more akin to the men's game.

Norwegian forward Ada Hegerberg has done just that. A prolific striker – she has scored 220 goals in 182 games in all competitions for Lyon at the time of writing – she is the Champions League record goalscorer and was the first player to win the women's Ballon d'Or in 2018. In 2019 she scored a hat-trick in just sixteen minutes as Lyon ripped apart Barcelona in the Champions League final. With a host of sponsorship deals she is one of the most marketable players in Europe but is also not afraid to use her platform to speak out against inequality, a move that has seen her step back from the Norwegian women's national team because she was unhappy with the support for women's and girls' football in the country.

'Obviously, I play football because I play football, and that's what I want to do,' she tells me.

But this is the sport I love and I really want us to push the sport in the right direction and leave it in a better place than it was when I got into it. Obviously you have a choice; you could play on and that's it. But I think when you reach a certain level a

*lot of responsibility comes with it. It's important to say that you
have to perform too, because if you don't perform, you don't
have a voice and then you won't have the same impact. Fact. So
that's kind of been my biggest motivation from day one; I train
every day to perform and also give myself a voice.*

The modern sporting superstar is increasingly vocal on
social issues and the sport they want to see. Just as players
such as Hegerberg have seen it as a necessity to speak up, so
Serena Williams, Simone Biles, Gabby Douglas, Sue Bird,
Naomi Osaka and plenty more have taken on the activist/
athlete role, in many cases having been thrust into the limelight by circumstances not of their own making, rather than
seeking it.

The current US women's national team is perhaps top of
that pile. And with twenty-six players involved in an ongoing
lawsuit against US Soccer over equal pay it is again perhaps
unfair to pick out one or two when all have been very
vocal on the dispute and what they want from the game. No
player, though, has become as adept at using their platform
to fight social injustice as Megan Rapinoe. As Hegerberg
said to me: 'Rapinoe should gain a lot of respect from other
footballers around the world because she's kind of took a
beating for all of us and the game, and we need strong voices
like that in order to push the game into the right direction.'

From taking a knee in support of Colin Kaepernick, to
raising money for communities devastated by wildfires, to
speaking out on LGBTQ+ rights, to challenging FIFA and
US Soccer to do more to grow the women's game, Rapinoe
is one of the most powerful athletes on the planet. An

incredible 2019 World Cup elevated her onto another plane, resulting in her winning the Ballon d'Or and FIFA's The Best FIFA Women's Player award. This additional visibility only increases her desire to use her platform to grow the game and change the world:

What am I trying to do ultimately? What are we trying to do? I think that everybody has a personal responsibility to do what they can to make the world a better place in the most impactful way that they can. This is it. This is the moment. And I'm so aware and understand that. I'm not just winning all these awards because I had a great year. It's the culmination of it all. And so with that comes so many other people; it comes with the team and what we've been able to do and the way we are organised and the way we fight together on and off the field; it comes from Colin Kaepernick; it comes from #MeToo and all of these other movements. It's very clear that I am a culminating moment of all of this that's happening right now. So for me to get on a stage and just thank family and friends would be so weird. It would seem so strange; I hesitate to say it but it would feel inauthentic.

What a privilege and an honour it is for me to sort of be the mouthpiece in this culminating moment. It is a big responsibility and I do feel a responsibility to take care of it and to give props and thanks and call out the people who could very well be in that position also.

The more that you can bring people in, that just starts this ripple effect. If I'm just talking about stuff for me, or just talking about one little specific thing or whatever, then it's like: this is limiting. I feel like the more I actually open it up the bigger it gets.

17 – The elephant in the room

Research by Nielsen shows a healthy 45 per cent of the population would consider watching women's sport live, compared with 63 per cent for men's sport. Yet for all the growing interest and increased investment, one main issue persists for the Women's Super League, as for many others worldwide: putting bums on seats.

Cracking attendances is the key to growing the game. Unlocking healthy crowds in turn unlocks the safe. It is the only way we will see wages and investment rise, negative attitudes smashed, and women's teams become a sustainable, indispensable arm of clubs.

Low attendances are also an often trotted-out criticism of the women's game. On social media, in comment sections, in pubs, regardless of context, you will see or hear, 'If more people watched or cared then things would be more equal' or, 'More people watch the National League than watch women's football.' And, beneath the veneer of vitriol to some comments, these are valid points worth answering.

It is hard to disagree: attendances *are* low – staggeringly so. Women's football has lower week-by-week averages than some sports with a fraction of the funding. The figures have been slowly climbing and received a boost in the wake of the success of the 2019 World Cup, but they are still, on average, low.

In 2015 the average attendance was 1,076; in 2016 it was 1,128. Following the switch from a summer to a winter season – mirroring the men's calendar – there was an 11 per cent drop to 953 fans per match. In the 2018–19 season that dip was almost clawed back, to an average of 1,010. But we're splitting hairs. The growth, the dips, were measured in tens. New fans were not being attracted to the game.

After being held back by the fifty-year ban from 1921, women's football was a sport with the potential for rapid and wide-ranging growth, and had the ability to become a very lucrative industry. Euro 2017 attracted a TV audience of 150 million, 43,423 were at Wembley for the 2018 Women's FA Cup final, and 43,264 the following year. The final of Mexico's new Liga MX Femenil in 2018 had 51,211 show up.

Why, then, was the potential not being realised domestically in England?

The overwhelming majority of WSL teams do not play in or particularly near their club's main ground. This requires a significant travel commitment from fans. The switch to a calendar more akin to the men's has also meant that fan bases are now being asked to commit their entire weekend to football should they want to follow both the women's and the men's teams. Bringing women's teams closer to clubs' spiritual homes is not straightforward, particularly in bigger cities. Land in and around London, for example, is expensive and undoubtedly hard to come by at the scale required for new mini-grounds for women's teams.

Manchester City provide the best set-up in the top flight by far. The Academy Stadium, a stone's throw from the Etihad Stadium, is a well-connected and purpose-built ground shared with the reserve and academy teams. Chelsea are perhaps a close second, with Kingsmeadow further from Stamford Bridge, being based in Norbiton, but nonetheless a fully branded and accessible stadium with strong advertising around it and around Fulham.

The decision of clubs to seriously invest, to discuss respective men's and women's calendars in the same conversations and to treat their women's teams as a serious arm of their business comes down to how clubs view the women's game – whether as a philanthropic effort, one based on public image, or as a viable commercial prospect.

If clubs were run in the interest of their fans and the wider communities they serve, it would be very different. Supporter-owned Championship side Lewes FC, whose men's and women's team play on the same pitch and receive equal funding and resources, provide a glimpse of what is possible. But the ownership model of most clubs means that the existence of women's domestic football, in its present form, is reliant on the potentially volatile whims of rich businessmen.

Helping attendances take a qualitative leap is not an easy task. Some have argued that small crowds in big grounds is not good for the players, atmosphere or televised coverage. They have a point, but the momentum of the game has shifted things. If playing in a big stadium means, at the very least, doubling those watching – increasing gate takings and visibility for sponsors – it is worth it.

In the 2019–20 season we saw the first meaningful jump in average attendances in the WSL era, to 3,072 fans. Fans weren't suddenly travelling to the out-of-reach home grounds of many teams; this was a direct result of the decision of clubs – post-2019 World Cup and with impetus from the FA – to host games in their main stadiums. On the opening weekend of the season 31,213 filed into the Etihad to watch City play United in a first WSL Manchester derby. That same weekend 24,564 showed up at Stamford Bridge to see Chelsea beat Tottenham. Later in the season 24,790 saw Tottenham beat West Ham at the London Stadium and a league record 38,262 watched the North London derby at the new Tottenham stadium.

This phenomenon, of bigger stadiums and bigger attendances, is not unique to England. In the same season 48,212 spectators were at San Mamés for Athletic Bilbao's 2–0 defeat by Atlético Madrid. Seven weeks later, 60,739 fans filed into the Wanda Metropolitano to watch Atlético take on their title rivals Barcelona, breaking the ninety-nine-year record for a domestic women's league game of 53,000, set by Dick, Kerr Ladies against St Helens on Boxing Day 1920.

In addition to those in situ in Madrid for the record match, 330,000 watched the match on the free-to-air channel Gol TV, peaking at 413,000. That figure was 4.27 per cent of the total audience share and the biggest viewing figure on Gol that week.

Bigger attendances are also not unique to football. England Netball, in a presentation to UK Sport in 2019, said: 'Our venue selections have grown from small sports hall facilities with under 1,000 people in attendance, to now selling out large arenas including the SSE Arena, Wembley, the Genting Arena, Echo Arena and the Copper Box.'

And, at the end of August 2019, England Rugby announced that the final of three Red Roses' Tests would see the women's team play Ireland at Twickenham, following the conclusion of a men's game against Australia. Other sports, not beholden to the might of the Premier League and football clubs with other, bigger interests, are able to experiment much more easily.

These may be one-off showpiece games, picked for their marketability, but they all suggest that an 'if you build it, they will come' mentality has started to develop. Accessible grounds, the chance to attend big stadiums cheaply, and top-level football are ripe conditions for any marketing team to be working with, as the 2019–20 season showed. But they need to go beyond marketing; the FA and clubs need to be campaigning for the crowds.

The majority of the record attendances of recent years were helped by promotions, such as free tickets for kids and season-ticket holders, while offers to local clubs and schools are the norm. At the Wanda for Atlético's big game it was no different, though of that record attendance, 26,912 (44 per cent) bought a ticket at €5–€10. Further promotion for that game included increased media, buses driving round the city with the faces of the women's team on the side, player signings at the club's store ahead of the match and the unveiling of three commemorative plaques for players who had reached one hundred caps. Beyond social media, this is the kind of active campaigning that is needed to help grow attendances.

The COVID-19 pandemic fundamentally altered the landscape of the women's game and the prism through which we viewed and analysed it – just as it did to every aspect of society across the world. In March 2020, as the rumblings of impending restrictions grew louder, I was in the US to watch the Lionesses compete at that year's SheBelieves Cup – a friendly tournament hosted by the US each year which England had won prior to the 2019 World Cup. In many respects we were a world away from the news in England, with the US a little behind the developments back home. But increasingly it felt like the shadow of the pandemic was creeping along behind us. Shortly after we had left Orlando, where the first two games were played, for New Jersey, the theme parks started to shut down. As we left from Newark Airport for Dallas for the final round of games New York was preparing to lock down and cases were on the rise. On the day we landed in Dallas the first positive cases were confirmed in Frisco, just north of Dallas, where the games would be played. On returning to England, our sold-out flight was half empty at best as US citizens pulled out amid fears they wouldn't be able to get back to the States if they travelled.

I landed at Heathrow on 12 March and football was suspended the following day. The impact of the pandemic on clubs dominated the sports news. No area of society was immune: there have been casualties in every sphere of life. Football was no different. Women's football was no different.

Clubs at the top of the men's game stood to lose millions in broadcast money and gate receipts. Clubs at the bottom, without the capital of those at the top, would likely crumble without tickets being sold. The FA faced huge losses too. With purse-tightening going on across the board, there were huge fears for the future of women's football.

FIFPRO, the global players' union, warned that the women's game was faced with an 'existential threat'. In a report it called on governing bodies and the game's stakeholders from across the world to step up, protect players and aspire 'to build a more solid foundation'. The report issued a stark warning that 'unless there is a clear commitment to stabilise competitions and provide financial assistance to keep leagues, clubs and players in business, the economic standstill will ultimately result in insolvencies of otherwise profitable and stable clubs'.

For the majority of women's teams, turnstile and other match-day income does not cover the cost of ground contracts or hire, staffing and travel. The broadcast rights for the women's game were then owned by BT Sport and BBC Sport, who did not pay for the rights to the games. This meant that postponements would be significantly less impactful to women's teams. The biggest losses would be felt covering player, coaching and staff contracts through a delayed and then cancelled season.

The women's game faced the same questions as the men's. Who would win the league? Who would get a Champions League place? Who would get relegated or promoted? But the financial implications of those decisions, or that of a voided season, whilst potentially devastating in the more fragile ecosystem of the women's game, were insignificant by comparison.

There was pressure on the FA to maintain a united stance on the resumption, or not, of professional football, across the Premier League, EFL, Women's Super League and Women's Championship. Split things up and they could be accused of mixed messages at a time when clarity in society was most sought after.

There was widespread sympathy towards the situation the FA was having to deal with. However, the delay in making a decision over the future of the season saw clubs, players, fans and all associated with the women's game increasingly frustrated. When they did eventually agree to cancel the season and award league positions based on points per game, despite the men's game being able to resume, there was widespread condemnation.

Ultimately, though, the pandemic exposed, and is still exposing to some extent, what lies beneath the shiny veneer of the WSL.

Calling the WSL a full-time fully professional league is not a lie, but it is a stretching of the truth, and the media are as guilty as the FA in the distortion because by hyping it you can help to grow it to the point where it actually becomes real. You help attract sponsors, you help attract the best players, you help attract the biggest audiences. The downside is that when the boat is rocked – by an unprecedented global pandemic, say – suddenly the temporary half-truths are fairly brutally exposed.

The return of women's professional football for the 2020–21 season was even more complicated than that of the men's game. Not because the will to bring it back was lacking, but because the base level of what professionalism means was a whole lot lower and interpreted by clubs in different ways.

Cancellation was not the only way. While it was widely reported that players and clubs in the WSL and Championship did not want to see out the remainder of the season, there were serious questions to be asked about the role that the FA, the Premier League and Premier League clubs played in paving the way for cancellation.

In Germany, two weeks after the resumption of the men's Bundesliga, and in the same week the fate of the WSL and Championship was confirmed, the Frauen-Bundesliga season resumed. The DFB and DFL – the German FA and the league, respectively – pulled together to provide support across the sport, including to the elite women's game. In England, the Premier League, to which the FA had been touting the running of the WSL, initially showed no such solidarity (it would eventually hand over £1 million to help cover the cost of the coronavirus testing programme ahead of the new season).

Suggesting similar measures to Germany for the English game felt extreme, radical and unrealistic in England generally. Why? Because the culture of football in England is very different to that in Germany. Privatisation has been a core component of government agendas for decades, under both Labour and Conservative governments, in England and there has been a conscious undermining of the idea of public ownership and investment. The short-term spending required to complete the season safely came with the warning that there could be long-term financial implications. The idea that there could have been ways to generate new income or push the biggest Premier League clubs into making the same financial sacrifices as those in the Bundesliga for the greater good and health of the game, and in the name of equality, did not seem to have ever been on the table in England.

The FA and Premier League talk the talk when it comes to equality and 'football for all' but when it mattered most it seemed as though an asterisk was attached with a footnote saying 'unless it asks questions of the might and morals of the market-driven Premier League'.

Before the season was cut short, clubs in the WSL and Championship were asked whether they could possibly meet the necessary safety requirements to finish the season and whether they had the financial resources to do so. It was the opposite of German solidarity, with the onus on individual clubs to magic their way through the crisis. That had an effect on morale. If clubs feared they could not provide a safe environment, and players felt their clubs could not do so unaided, of course they were going to favour cancellation.

The lack of financial support, the lengthy period of uncertainty and an unwillingness to bring football's resources together to navigate the crisis meant the feedback to the FA's questions would go only one way, because it had been engineered to make completion unviable, risky and scary.

The same conversations took place after the first lockdown had ended around the closure of girls' academies. No one wanted to see academies closed, but when the government announced a lockdown, according to the FA academies did not meet the 'necessary "elite" protocols'. The announcement was made within days of the shut-out beginning, meaning there was little wriggle room for clubs to redress the inequities in their academy systems to bring the level up to 'elite' standards or for the FA to redress the rules that allowed those inequalities to exist in the first place.

One club managed to announce an intent to reopen its academy – Brighton having said that its girls' Duel Career Academy would be able to resume as it operated under the same protocols as its boys' academy. A few others would eventually follow suit.

Once again the pandemic had exposed inequalities – such as the use of non-club pitches, poorer facilities generally, fewer staff, less access to medical facilities – that had, to some extent, been hushed up because overall progress was being made.

Should that progress happen faster? No doubt. There is plenty of money swilling around for clubs to be able to pro-vide mirroring pathways and contracts for boys and girls, pandemic or no pandemic.

The full impact of the pandemic on the grassroots and amateur levels of the game will be impossible to tell for some time yet. At the top end, the return of the WSL and Championship in 2020–21 was surprisingly successful. Five USWNT stars joined for the season to ensure they got play-ing time ahead of the Tokyo Olympics, with football in the US shrouded in uncertainty following the successful but short NWSL Challenge Cup.* Alex Morgan joined Tottenham, Christen Press and Tobin Heath moved to Manchester United, and Rose Lavelle and Sam Mewis joined Manchester City. With European Player of the Year Pernille Harder having joined Chelsea in the summer too there was huge optimism around the restart and the potential of the leagues.

---

* A bubbled competition that was the first live sport to return to action in the US, attracting huge viewing figures and a raft of new sponsors.

Sue Campbell summed up one of the more surprising effects of the pandemic, saying:

It gave us all time to think. Which might sound like a strange thing to say, but there's been more progress on some areas in the last six months than I've seen in four years, because people have actually had time to think, to talk and to drive ideas forward.

We've actually, interestingly, got more interest in the game. The only place I think it might have set us back or where sport has been set back generally is at the grassroots end. I don't know, for example, what the real impact will be on kids who have not had PE or sport for a while. We know, when you look at the stats the Youth Sport Trust have brought out, that kids from socio-economically deprived areas had less exercise, less everything frankly. I was listening to the CEO of Ofsted, she was saying that there is a massive drop-off in kids' writing and concentrating, I'm sure that's true in sport too. We won't measure it the same, but I'm sure it's there. I worry about that. I worry about the impact on just basic physical activity. Then I really worry about our clubs and all those mini soccer centres; it started, it stopped, it started, it stopped again. I am worried for grassroots; it's going to take some real hard work to reignite.

It varies right across the board. Has it set us back years? I don't think so. Set us back? Definitely, in different parts. But I'm a great believer that the great human race is very resilient. Once we get cracking again, as long as we make it exciting and interesting and attractive, we'll get people back. Women's football survived a fifty-year ban, it will survive a pandemic.

That is a great way of contextualising the resilience of women's football and the resilience of the people that care about it. The FA undoubtedly made some mistakes in the way they handled the pandemic but when the pace of events is so swift, and the scenario so unfamiliar, it is easier to be a little forgiving of some of those errors made while running and unable to catch a breath.

The fragility of women's football being exposed is also a good thing. The FA had built the house without building the foundations in the hope that the more interest there was in the shiny attractive house, the better able and resourced they would be to add the foundations later without anyone noticing. It was a risk. A global pandemic coming along to shake the house would not have been high on the list of likely scenarios when they were looking at potential pitfalls.

The pandemic would further highlight the risks that come with bonding the women's game so closely with the men's game too. Project Big Picture was a plan cooked up by Liverpool and Manchester United that would see the power in the Premier League concentrated into the hands of the so-called 'big six' of Liverpool, Manchester United, Manchester City, Arsenal, Tottenham and Chelsea – plus West Ham, Everton and Southampton – in exchange for a £100 million gift to the FA to help it deal with its £300 million financial hit due to the COVID-19 pandemic.

It was forced to be shelved soon after the details were leaked. Six months later and twelve of the biggest teams in Europe – Real Madrid, Barcelona, Atlético Madrid, Juventus, Inter Milan, AC Milan, Arsenal, Liverpool, Manchester City, Manchester United, Chelsea and Tottenham – would attempt an even more audacious coup for greater financial control and stability by announcing the launch of a European Super League. Both projects used the pandemic to plead poverty and the need for these new plans but both had been in the planning long before COVID squeezed pockets. It was only thanks to the backlash from fans that both collapsed.

What both projects did, though, was threaten to drag women's football along with them. Project Big Picture promised £10 million to bail out the WSL and Women's Championship, a commitment that 'a new independent league for the women's professional game will finally be developed and funded' and more than £50 million a year for the WSL, Championship, Women's FA Cup and grass-roots – dwarfing the £11 million the FA put into women's football in 2019.

Meanwhile, the European Super League assured that: 'As soon as practicable after the start of the men's competition, a corresponding women's league will also be launched, help-ing to advance and develop the women's game.'

Reduced to a single sentence, with no further informa-tion on what that means or how it would work, it seems a foregone conclusion that the women's teams will simply follow the men's.

The problem is the twelve teams involved were not representative of the elite of European women's football. They held one Champions League trophy between them (although Barcelona have since won a first European title). The clubs of the three owners quoted in the press release, a trio understood to be driving this plan forward, had historically not been interested in women's football at all:

Manchester United's team was three years old, Juventus's four (despite a rich history of support for the women's game in the 1970s), while Real Madrid were playing their first season in the Primera Iberdrola.

Liverpool, drivers of the doomed Project Big Picture had, as we have discussed, built a state-of-the-art training ground with no room for their women's team, who failed to earn promotion back to the Women's Super League after being relegated in the 2019–20 season.

Meanwhile, Lyon – the champions of Europe, seven-time winners of the Champions League – and German champions Wolfsburg, twice winners of the tournament, sat outside the pack.

If the women's game had been dragged along for the ride the consequences would have been huge. Equally, if the ESL launch had not included this token nod the effects on the women's game would probably have been as detrimental. In many ways the ESL debacle offered a warning of where the profit motive will take the game and, for women's football, where being aligned with the men's game could lead.

Women's football is riding the crest of a wave, but in the drive to rapidly progress and secure the finances for clubs to maintain professional and semi-professional teams it has been tied ever closer to the model of the men's Premier League and to men's Premier League clubs.

For the majority of its existence women's football has relied on goodwill and trust, which worked when there was nothing financial to be gained from involvement in the game. Now, with increasing sponsorship deals, the

Barclays league sponsorship and the WSL broadcast-rights deal between Sky Sports and BBC Sport, it is inevitable the vultures will start to circle.

The potential of women's football to bring a return, in the medium to long term, is an idea that has been put to clubs and sponsors to encourage them into the fold. That is not necessarily a bad thing; investment is important if the game is to grow. But there is an increasing need to be more alert to the risks involved when individuals or organisations put their interests above the broader development of the game.

Women's football needs to protect itself from self-interest and examine the structures designed to safeguard its future. Two questions need to be asked after the ESL mess. First, how can women's football avoid being affected by ESL-style manoeuvring in the men's game? And second, how can it forge a different path to the profit-at-all-costs route taken by the men's game?

Conclusion: A manifesto

In the countries where it is strongest, women's football is now at a critical juncture. In England, Barclays' sponsorship of the league is up for renewal. With a historic broadcast deal meaning games are now aired on the BBC and Sky week in week out, the title rights to the league are undoubtedly worth more than they were previously.

In the Champions League, a game-changing redistribution model came in at the start of the 2020–21 season, promising more money for competing clubs, solidarity payments to clubs in leagues with teams involved in the European competition and £10 million from the men's Champions League for the women's.

All points to the potential of the women's game. But there are also many reasons to be cautious. If one thing is to be learned from the men's game, it is that it cannot be taken on trust that club owners and financial institutions care about football. There are not enough safeguarding measures to protect women's football from being exploited and to make sure that money coming in goes back into building it from the bottom up.

In fact there is even less accountability in the WSL and Championship than in the Premier League. The FA board has members from six clubs to represent the twenty-three teams in the top two divisions. Of the six, four are WSL clubs and two Championship clubs. Five of the six are attached to men's

Premier League sides. All four WSL club representatives were part of the 'dirty dozen' – those involved in the European Super League.

It is also not people directly involved in the day-to-day running of women's teams that sit on the board. How can individuals with primary business interests in the men's game be expected to understand the nuances of what it's like for Lewes or Charlton, for example, and why should they care? There is no one-member-one-vote rule like there is in the Premier League, where two-thirds must agree changes. There are huge problems with the Premier League model, where each club is a shareholder, but the fact that women's football is less democratic is worrying.

Fan representation and ownership are often cited as key checks on clubs. In the women's game the fan movement is in its infancy and needs to be developed fast. It also needs to be taken seriously and should be brought into structures, not kept on the sidelines as cheerleader or volunteer wings of clubs.

There is so much to love about women's football. So many differences to be celebrated. Women's football is more inclusive. Yes, there have been incidents of racism and homophobia – as we have repeatedly seen, football doesn't exist in a bubble and all the ills of society are re-flected within it. However, given you already must have a certain progressive streak in you to have supported women's football and seen the value in it to date, the arena is overall more progressive. That will change as more fans are drawn in and the sample size is bigger and more diverse, but the fact that there is a culture of inclusivity at the core of the game, with gay players being out, proud and vocal advocates for LGBTQ+ rights and known for challenging inequality, will help prevent the ills of society from infecting it too deeply.

Players have needed fans to help justify their right to be able to build a career from the game, which has resulted in a closeness between fans and players that you do not see in the men's game. After every fixture players will spend up to an hour, sometimes more, talking to fans, signing autographs and taking photos, rain or shine. This has in part been helped by the many years of the game being part time and amateur in nature. Players have the same struggles as fans. The overwhelming majority live fairly modestly and still wonder how they will pay the bills. As fans, we want the game to professionalise. We want the game to be able to provide a good standard of living for players and provide for them long term. We don't want players to have to wonder where the money will come from should they get injured or when they retire.

A key question moving forward will be how we can maintain the connection with fans as the game grows, as demands on players' time get greater and star status is reached as a result of increased coverage and sponsorships. In some respects 'Dubai-gate' – when a handful of players escaped to Dubai amid the travel restrictions of December 2020, while most people (including amateur-level players) were struggling at home with uncertain employment, home-schooling children and all the precariousness of the pandemic – sounded a small warning of the potential for a disconnect with fans to develop.

The irony is that in many ways it is a marker of progress that players can now afford to holiday in Dubai and command some of the lifestyle awarded to their male counterparts. On that occasion, however, they massively misread the room, and it is hard to overstate the fissures caused in the relationship between fans and players at the elite end at the time. It was one of the first displays of the type of entitlement and privilege we've almost become numbed to in the men's game.

But beyond the negative question of how we avoid the excesses of the men's game is a much more interesting one. How can we build a better game? How can we take the best aspects of both sides of the sport in order to create something truly reflective of society and deeply embedded within it?

In 2020, protests would push the Scottish government into making period products free in public buildings, schools and universities. Hundreds of thousands protested in Poland after the Constitutional Court effectively banned abortion by saying it was unconstitutional in cases of severe foetal abnormalities – when such cases accounted for 96 per cent of legal abortions. Women would be central to the Black Lives Matter protests around the world, with #SayHerName used to highlight the deaths of Breonna Taylor, Sandra Bland and hundreds of other black women killed by police in the US. The brutal murder of Sarah Everard by PC Wayne Couzens after she disappeared when walking home from a friend's prompted vigils, protests and huge anger. This is the post-#MeToo era, where women are no long staying silent over abuses and inequalities.

In football women have been fighting too. For better playing facilities and conditions, for maternity rights, for equal pay and more. Scotland held a media blackout while in dispute with the Scottish FA over pay and conditions, Australian W-League players won a significant pay increase, Nigeria held a sit-in protest over unpaid allowances and bonuses, the Republic of Ireland national team threatened to strike, eight former Brazil players penned an open letter criticising their set-up and demanding greater respect, Denmark forfeited a game in a dispute over pay. In 2020 Brazil and Sierra Leone joined Australia, England, Norway and New Zealand in committing to equal pay for their women's and men's national teams. Members of the Afghanistan women's national team exposed the brutal sexual and physical abuses they had suffered at the hands of the president of the Afghanistan Football Federation. Iranian women have fought for the right to watch games.

The USWNT have been locked in a vicious legal battle with US Soccer over the unequal pay and conditions of the women's and men's national teams. Between 2016 and 2018 the women's games generated approximately $900,000 more revenue for US Soccer than the men's games. After the 2015 World Cup win that figure reached $1.9 million. In 2021 a judge approved a partial settlement deal on working conditions – which included flights, hotels, venue selection and staffing – and, at the time of writing, the team were in the process of appealing the court's rejection of their equal pay claim.

The time is right for women's football to be shaped in the way we want to see it. In many countries not covered in this

221

book, in Africa and Latin America, for example, there are also huge opportunities for the growth of the game and for the game to have a broader impact on societies' perceptions on equality. Women's football needs bold and innovative leadership to navigate this period. In England it increasingly seems like the FA is unable to provide that leadership. Why? Because, despite some extremely talented and passionate staff working with the best of intentions, women's football cannot help but be shackled by the FA's other commitments.

For a while now, the FA has touted the idea of handing the WSL over to the Premier League to run. Early in 2020 Premier League clubs were presented with a feasibility study into a potential takeover but kicked the decision into the long grass, agreeing to have another look in a year. At the time, the FA said that it was 'supporting the Premier League in a project to explore the long-term feasibility of the Premier League running the Women's Super League. This is a purely exploratory project and based on a long-term timescale.'

Despite the constant tinkering with the leagues, with mixed results and many casualties, there can be little doubt that the decision of the FA to invest more seriously in the women's game in recent years has resulted in huge strides on the pitch as well as off it. It has given the women's game more authority in the eyes of the public, sponsors and broadcasters. Women's football in England needed the FA.

Yet there is an argument that the FA has taken the women's game as far as it can. That, with the Premier League wielding the real power in English football and the FA unable to make decisions solely in the interests of the women's game, it can no longer drive the next stage of development with the ruthlessness needed in this most un-forgiving of industries.

That isn't to say that a Premier League takeover would be any better – quite the opposite, in fact. This pandemic has shown the selfishness and greed of the men's top tier in all its ignominy. Just as women's football is not the FA's sole priority, nor would it be the top priority of the Premier League. The way football is run and structured in England means the women's game would always play second fiddle to the men's.

Another option on the table is to have the league supported and run by private-equity investors. The clear moral of the European Super League and Project Big Picture stories, how-ever, is that short-term gain comes at a price, and one that is usually detrimental to the heart and soul of football.

One answer could be for English football to rethink its purpose and push closer to how Germany does things. Another could lie in independent leadership – a body that can run the women's game, both the WSL and Champion-ship, and make decisions solely in its interest.

We just have to look Stateside for a glimpse of what that could look like. The National Women's Soccer League was managed by US Soccer until the clubs, which own the league, negotiated a structured separation. This means the league will be run independently of the federation but with ongoing financial support while it works towards sustainable independence. The NWSL is not perfect, but during the pandemic it found a way to fight its corner and became the first professional team sport to return in the US. Sponsorship deals could have easily become casualties of the pandemic but the NWSL found a way to keep itself attractive – Budweiser, CBS, Nike, P&G, Secret, Thorne, Twitch and Verizon all backed the bubbled Challenge Cup tournament.

The WSL has the authority and profile to tread the same path. It is attractive in its own right and a leadership structure making decisions unhindered could be very effective in this market-driven game.

Independence and sustainability are key. Increasingly it is hard to see a healthy future for the women's game if teams stay so beholden to the men's sides. However, no club that has invested with one eye on a potential future bonanza return is going to relinquish control of their women's side just as the game is showing early signs of profitability. They will want a piece of the pie and, perhaps more significantly, will not want the women's game to champion a more progressive and fairer way of doing things.

Independence and sustainability, if achievable, are not all that is needed; the way women's football is governed needs to change too. It may sound radical, but whether clubs should be run completely independently of parent clubs should be a serious consideration.

Could or should men's clubs be forced to break from their women's teams and be made to pay into a central pot of funding to the WSL that is distributed equally instead of individual clubs being funded at the whim of their owners? It would guard against clubs in financial trouble cutting from the women's side first, would ensure women's teams are run with their interests as a priority and would create a more level playing field.

For Ada Hegerberg, equality has to start at the bottom:

*When we start from the beginning – we are talking about
young girls and young boys – the condition should be exactly
the same because there's no profit in the game. So why isn't it
the case that young girls get the same pitches to get the same
confidence as the young boys get?*

*In the end, if you want to see a good product, then you
must start by taking those young girls seriously, from day
one, then they have a much, much better chance of creating
a good product. It's a vicious circle, because if you don't grab
the problem by its roots – and basically for me grabbing the
problem from the roots is by taking young girls seriously and
starting to train them in the same manner and putting the same
demands on them as you do with young boys – then you create
an inferior product and the gap gets big as you go up the age
groups.*

Megan Rapinoe thinks there is an argument to say we
should go one step further and invest more in women's football than men's to make up for the historic underfunding.
I agree. 'It's just basic common sense: over-invest in underserved communities otherwise the gap will just continue to
be exactly the same,' she says.

*In order to close the gap we have to double down. And also, it
can't be or shouldn't be looked at as a charity give. The potential
of women's football from a business perspective is massive. Imagine
if FIFA actually invested in the World Cup? I mean, it was huge,
but really an inadequate amount of investment. Imagine if they*

properly did the World Cup in France. They barely even had
merchandise; you couldn't get shit, it sold out. So there's just such
a missed opportunity and so much money left on the table.

Obviously with our Federation as well I'm like: 'Yes, we
want more money, of course, and we think we deserve to be paid
more, but also if we're making more money then you're making
money too and if we grow this thing together then everybody
eats.' The business opportunity is there.

Rapinoe also agrees that there are lessons to be taken from
the men's game, both in terms of what to do and what to
avoid at all costs:

We have this very mature product that we can look at and
take the things that we like and maybe leave the things that
we don't. All we can do is just try to make it better every day
and try to not make the same mistakes that the men's game has
made. Try to be interesting and inclusive when we're growing
the game and making policy, making rules and starting leagues.
We need to get everybody's perspective, get everybody's opinion,
have all the people in the room, so to speak, to get the best
product that you can that is the best for everyone, fans, teams,
players, everyone alike.

In many ways it is that simple. Currently there are not
enough women or other minority groups reflected in the
corridors of power. 'It's a serious problem,' says Rapinoe.

I always go back to this example of some beer company that
had an advertisement that lasted like about four minutes before

they pulled it that said, 'Take the "no" out of your night.' You're talking about rape here, and I feel like any woman in that room would have been like 'actually, you're going to want to keep the "nos" in there'. It's not that people are purposely overlooking things, it's that they literally do not think of it because it's not their perspective, it's not their experience. So that's the reason that we need diversity and inclusion, so you get the full picture, so you can then make the best product, have the best advert, do the best story, whatever it may be. That's the reason why you need it. Representation, if it's missing, you're not going to get the best product that you can get. I'm not saying that your product is bad, but it's not going to be the best.

Very few new businesses make money in their first year. As the saying goes, 'it takes money to make money'. If you spend and invest time and energy as well as finances then you give a product credibility and the interest builds. Time and time again, with every passing year, women's football is proving the demand is there.

I have benefited from that directly. When I was commissioned to begin the *Guardian*'s women's football column in June 2017 I was told we would need to review it in September to see how it was going. We never had that conversation. Why? Because an underserved audience was proving the demand. The stats were good. Two years later I was writing full time on women's football in a post that didn't exist anywhere when I began. That's all it takes: commitment. Commitment from clubs and governing bodies to make decisions in the best interests of the sport and safeguard it. Commitment from the media. Commitment from fans. Commitment from clubs both financially but also logistically.

Put more women's games in men's stadiums. Give them access to your best facilities. Even hosting the women's team twice a year in the main stadium would be transformative. Piggyback a men's fixture now and again – not to artificially inflate crowd sizes but to make your investment in women's football and the progress of the game as a whole significantly more accessible to your most loyal fans. Sell them the game. Arrange free or subsidised travel when playing at the less accessible grounds. Motivate the commitment you are hoping fans will make in the long term. Until clubs start to fully embrace the potential that exists, the game will be shackled and so will the consciousness of the population. If teams want fans to fully embrace, support and fall in love with women's football they have to show they back it and value it fully.

By backing the women's game sincerely clubs and governing bodies have an opportunity to go beyond football, to use the influence of the sport to push and grow the equality message in homes, schools and workplaces up and down the country – not in a confrontational way but by setting an example. It is only when we have real genuine equality and a society that puts the needs of people over profit more generally that we can start discussing the nuances of improving the game: whether goals or pitches should be smaller, to accommodate the physical differences of women (a discussion that would be pertinent on the men's side too given the physical changes in men's physiques since the rules of the game were written). Chelsea manager Emma Hayes explained it best when she told BT Sport:

There is often a criticism about goalkeeping in the women's game. I would argue that the goal is just a little bit too big; if it was built around our physical differences then we would be talking about great goalkeepers as opposed to exposing them.

Rather than mirror everything we take from the men's game, we have to adapt it to our own sport and our own physical expectations as well as the tactical implications.

It's the mindset that has to change, and once it starts to change, there is a realisation that the sport has its own differences because, more often than not, everyone coming into our game is coming from the men's game or other sports.

At present, it is not helpful, when access to pitches and basic facilities is difficult, to demand changes that would require huge investment and change. But in a fairer, more equal society, where sport is played for enjoyment, passion and exercise and not greed, we would be able to properly build it in its best form.

Women's football is an incredibly young game with the huge potential to develop into one of the biggest sports in the world. It is not shackled by the historical expectations that exist within the men's game or in many other sports. It has the opportunity to become a standard-bearer for positive change, and to inspire millions of people worldwide – regardless of gender — just as the factory teams inspired and brought together a nation in wartime, just as I was inspired by the likes of Kelly Smith when I was growing up, and just as Rapinoe, Hegerberg et al. continue to inspire today.

A vibrant and thriving women's game is commercially viable and entertaining but women's football is also hugely beneficial to society more widely. Team sports can have a big impact on the confidence and relationship-building of players and provide girls and women with skills that are invaluable in multiple walks of life. It is vital that growth at the top feeds back down into the grassroots game.

There is a huge amount of money in football. Governing bodies are not-for-profit organisations and women's football needs to be bold in asking for a bigger slice of the pie. The men's game did not develop in isolation: investment, financial and otherwise, led to its growth and success. Only when the level of support that has been afforded to the men's game is afforded to the women's – or greater, given we're playing catch-up – will we be able to realise the full potential of women's football.

We should think big. Why can't countries beyond the US implement Title IX-type legislation that doesn't allow the development of women's football at youth levels to be outstripped by the men's financially? Why can't prize pots at major tournaments such as the World Cup be matched between genders? Why can't women's games be given prime-time broadcast slots? Why can't there be proper safeguarding throughout football to protect the most vulnerable players, amateur or professional?

If there is one thing we can take from this potted history of the women's game it is that women footballers are resilient and effective fighters. We can achieve incredible things when driving for change together, not just with each other but by connecting literally or ideologically with the broader struggles of women and other groups, be they based on gender, race, sexuality or class. The opportunity is ours for the taking.

Acknowledgements

How do you even begin to thank people for getting you through a lengthy project like this? Particularly when the entire period of writing was dominated by a global pandemic that shut down access to archives, ended travel and reduced interviews to conversations over Zoom?

It feels impossible. As impossible as writing this book has felt at times – most of the time.

When the very enthusiastic literary agent Max Edwards of Aevitas Creative approached me about writing a book on the history of women's football it's fair to say I baulked at the idea. But the timing made sense, and the idea of writing a popular history of the women's game that looked to contextualise it within a history of society generally was appealing.

In many respects I hate Max for the two years that followed our tentative first discussion and in another very small way, which grew a little when I held the proofs in my hands and will perhaps grow further when I hold the finished article, I love him for making me do it. For that I begrudgingly thank him.

It is completely fair to say that without my much better half Michael and my son James, writing this book would have been unthinkable and being able to do my job, as a sport writer for the *Guardian* would be impossible. They bore, and continue to bear, the brunt of every late night working, of every trip away (sometimes for weeks on end), of every weekend or evening match and of every interrupted holiday and pick up the slack at home.

Behind them, supporting them in my absence, helping us juggle childcare and shift patterns is an immense network of close family that have to all be named just to make up for all the last-minute desperate pleas for babysitters. So here goes, much love and thanks to: Judy Beishon, Ian Turner, Dave Webb, Helen Hackworthy, Holly Hackworthy, Jack Hackworthy, Sally Beishon, Kyle Ansari, Ivy Beishon, Rosey Wrack, Mark Milligan, Matt Wrack, Sheila Wrack, Sarah Wrack, Danny Byrne, Cillian Byrne, Cheryl Wardley, Scott Wardley, John Weymouth, Shannon Norris, Phoebe Kendall-Micallef, Leli Kendall-Micallef, Kaycee Weymouth, John Weymouth and the rest of the Wracks, Beishons and extended family.

Powering me through the pandemic and the world of women's football with cynicism and laughter and listening to all my moaning about the book were the 'Margaritas' (Molly Hudson, Emma Sanders, Rachel O'Sullivan, Sophie Downey and Claire Bloomfield) and dynamic duo Maggie Murphy and Lucy Mills.

I owe an immense debt of gratitude to the *Guardian* for both giving me the time to write this beast and putting me in the position to be able to do it and to be considered to be the right person to write it in the first place. To Martin Rose and Philip Cornwall, who got me in to work on the production desk, to Anna Kessel, who recommended me when the desk were looking for a women's football writer, to Owen Gibson, the then head of sport that got me writing for the paper, to the production staff that put up with me on shift and now have to cope with my copy, to current head of sport Will Woodward for fighting for me, to Louise Taylor, who is the nicest person to share writing about women's football with, and finally to football editors Jon Brodkin and Marcus Christensen who genuinely give a damn about women's football. I couldn't be working with a better team.

My time at the *Guardian* wouldn't have begun without the brutal but sage advice of the late Vikki Orvice and her wonderful supportive husband and fellow journalist Ian Ridley who championed me early on.

I will be eternally grateful to Helena Ní Bhroin, Gary James and Kieran Theivam for going through this tomb and giving me utterly invaluable feedback.

To the team at Faber in the UK (including Fred Baty, Ruth O'Loughlin, Rachael Williamson, Donna Payne, Jack Murphy, Connor Hutchinson and Jess Kim) and Triumph in the US (including Noah Amstadter, Michelle Bruton, Jen DePoorter, Josh Williams and Clarissa Young), thank you for all you've done to bring this to fruition in extraordinary times and with me missing pretty much every deadline under the sun.

Finally, women's football. How can I possibly have more gratitude towards this beast of a game that captured my heart from an early age and has given me such a fulfilling career? I can't. I owe everyone that has fought for this game. Not least those that contributed to this book through interviews (Gail Newsham, Sue Campbell, Kelly Simmons, Megan Rapinoe, Ada Hegerberg, Jean-Michel Aulas, Louise Raw,

Anson Dorrance, Kay Cossington and others) and through their extensive and exhaustive research that was invaluable when writing this book (Jean Williams, Gary James, Stuart Gibbs, John Simkin, Steve Bolton, Helge Faller, Sue Lopez, Fiona Skillen and more).

This is a lot of thanks, but just as women's football doesn't exist in isolation, removed from the world around it, neither does the writer.

234

Photo credits

Index

A page number followed by 'n' indicates a footnote, e.g. 91n.

abortion 80, 130, 220
academies 169, 170, 174, 203, 210–11
ACF Milan 90
ACL (anterior cruciate ligament) injuries 177–8, 179–80
activism *see* protests and activism
Adams, Nicola 130–1
Afghanistan: abuse of players 221; national team 162, 221
Akers, Michelle 106, 107, 127, 193
Akers, Vic 119–21, 188
Aluko, Eni 152
Amazon Grimstad 114
Andonovski, Vlatko 166
Andreyivic, Mikelov 85
Argentina: national team 92, 95–6, 156; pay dispute 6–7
armed forces, women in 72–3
Arsenal: 1990s–2000s domination 119–21, 195–6; after school sessions 4; investment by men's side 120, 141–2, 169; wins place in WSL 169; other mentions 55–6, 61, 124, 144, 178, 188, 197–8
Ashley, Percy 74
Asian Football Confederation (AFC) 103, 104
Astor, Nancy 46
The Athletic 133–4
Athletic Bilbao 204
Atlético Madrid 204, 205
attendance at matches (recent years) 8, 201–5
Attlee, Clement 49

Augustesen, Susanne 91
Aulas, Jean-Michel 122–7
austerity measures, impact: on schools (UK) 140; on women 128–9
Australia: national team 104, 108, 165–6, 221; players' pay 221

Balliol, Carrie 17
bans on women's football: 1902 58; 1921 56–65; 1945 (Scotland) 74; 1970 ban lifting 82–6; media and public responses to 59–60, 61–2, 63, 64–5; other countries 66, 68, 92, 117; players' responses to 60–1, 63–4
Barcelona 198, 204
Barcs, Sándor 83
Bardsley, Karen 169
Bareman, Sarai 176–7
'Barnet Blazers' Ladies' satirical club rules 49–51
Barnet Press 49–51
Barton, Janice 95
Bassett, Laura 134
Batt, Harry 92, 95, 96
Bauwens, Peco 117
Bayern Munich 144
Beckett, Emma 178
Benjamin, Floella 140–1
Biles, Simone 199
Bird, Sue 199
Birkens, Miss (Dick, Kerr Ladies) 43
Birmingham 169, 174, 178

Bisanz, Gero 118
Black Lives Matter movement 220
Bland, Sandra 220
Blatter, Sepp 104
#BlueGirl 151
Bolton Ladies 72, 74
Bosnia and Herzegovina, national
    team 147
Brazier, Katie 184–5
Brazil: 1941-1981 ban on women's
    football 66; demand for greater
    respect for players 6–7, 221;
    national team 91, 104, 106, 131–2,
    196, 197, 221
Brazil, Ellie 178
Bright, Millie 145
Brighton 178, 190, 211
Brighton and Hove Albion 170
Bristol Academy 169
Bristol City 152
British Ladies' Football Club 22–6,
    30–2
broadcast rights and contracts 150,
    174, 175, 187, 206, 207, 216, 217
Bronze, Lucy 102, 155, 159, 160–1
Brunei, national team 131
Bryan, Gemma 177
Brymner, Minnie 17
Buckley, John 189
BUL, Oslo 114–15
Burke, Tarana 147
Bush, George 107
Byrne, Emma 121

Caleb, Leah 95
Cameroon, national team 155, 156–7,
    158–9
Campbell, Sue 136, 137, 142, 161–2,
    171–2, 185–6, 212
Canada: 2015 hosts World Cup 132;
    ban on women's football 68;
    national team 104, 105, 108, 111,
    132, 155, 166

Caribbean, 1960 hosts Corinthians
    and Nomads 74
Carlisle, Alexander 14
Carney, Karen 134
Carter, Danielle 178
Carter, Haley 162
Cassell, Dot 90
Castle, Barbara 80
Champions League, women's
    (formerly UEFA Women's Cup)
    119, 121, 122, 124, 196, 198, 210
Chapman, Katie 121
charity matches: First World War
    38–9, 40–4; inter-War years
    48–56, 63, 69–71, 72, 114; post
    Second World War 74–5
Charles, George Fredrick 17
Charlton 189
Chastain, Brandi 193
Chelsea: investment by men's
    side 122, 141–2, 169, 170, 203;
    wins place in WSL 169; other
    mentions 120, 152, 184, 204, 211
childcare provision: closure of Sure
    Start centres 130; Second World
    War 79; US 47
Chile, national team 165
China: 1988 hosts international
    invitational tournament 104–5;
    1991 hosts first Women's World
    Cup 105–6; Chunghua Cup 103;
    cuju ('kickball') 14–15; national
    team 104–5, 106, 166
Chinese Taipei Football Association
    (CTFA) 103, 106
Chunghua Cup 103
Churchill, Winston 46, 49
Civil Rights Act (1964) 99
Clayton, E. (Preston Ladies) 70
Closing the Gap (FA) 186–7
clothing and kit: ancient China, cuju
    players 15; 19th century 15–16, 18,
    19, 20, 25, 31; early 20th century

(comic costume) 33; First World War 38, 41–2; post First World War 50, 51; 1971 second unofficial Women's World Cup 93; 2000s 123–4; 2010s 124

Cole, Louise 16, 17

college sport (US) 100–1, 194

Collingwood, Paul 146

Collins, Patrick Joseph 65

Colombia, national team 6–7, 132

Confederation of African Football (CAF) 104

Confederation of North, Central America and Caribbean Association Football (CONCACAF) 104

contraception and sexual health 47, 79, 98

Cook, Elsie 90

Copeland, Ted 110, 111

Coppa del Mondo (1970) 89, 92

Corinthian Ladies 74–5, 90, 171

Corriere dello Sport 92

Cossington, Kay 102

Coulthard Ladies 41–3

Couzens, Wayne 220

COVID-19 pandemic 164, 165, 166, 173, 205–13, 219–20, 223–4

cricket, women's 146

Croydon 119

Crystal Palace 177, 178, 189

cuju ('kickball,' ancient China 14–15

Czechoslovakia, national team 104, 117

Daily Mirror 86, 96

Daily Sketch 6

Davenport, Eva 17

De Haro, Jaime 93

Dein, David 120

Denmark: 1970 wins first unofficial Women's World Cup 89, 92; 1980s size of women's football 91n; national team 89, 92, 106, 112, 146; pay dispute 6–7, 221; women's rights and equality 113–14

Dennerby, Thomas 157

Derby County 189

Derby Daily Telegraph 52

Dick, Kerr Ladies (later Preston Ladies) 39–44, 48, 51–6, 60–1, 64–5, 67–72, 191–2, 204

Dixie, Lady Florence 22, 24, 25, 32

Doncaster Rovers Belles ('Donny Belles') (previously Doncaster Belles) 119, 169, 185–6, 188–9

Donk, Daniëlle van de 144, 145

Dorrance, Anson 100–2, 106–8, 194

Dorries, Nadine 130

Douglas, Gabby 131, 199

Drogba, Didier 1

'Dubai-gate' 219–20

Duel Career Academy, Brighton 211

Duisberg 119

Dundee Evening Telegraph 52–3

Dunfermline Journal 18

Dunn, Crystal 148

Durham 183

East Kent Times and Mail 85

Edinburgh City Girls 72

Edinburgh Lady Dynamos 74

Ejangue, Augustine 158

employment equality 113, 128 *see also* equal pay

Emslie, Claire 155

Engen, Ingrid 156

England: academies 169, 170, 174, 203, 210–11; cricket 146; hosts 2005 Euros 148–9; hosts 2012 Olympics 130–2; national team *see* England national team; netball 204; players' pay equality 221; professionalism 7, 120, 141–2, 169–70, 173–4, 177–90, 198, 208, 219–20; racism scandal 152; rugby

205; school and youth football 3–4, 138–41, 145; vs Scotland, 19th century matches 4–5, 15–21; Team GB 130–2, 165–6; Women's Championship 170, 182, 186, 189–90, 203, 211, 214, 223; Women's Premier League 110, 121, 183 *see also* Football Association (FA); Women's Football Association (WFA); Women's Super League (WSL); *specific teams*

England national team: 1960s-1970s 89, 90, 92, 95–6, 193; 1990s 108–9, 110–11; 2010s 132–5, 143, 145, 146, 147–8, 152, 153–4, 155, 156, 158–9, 160–2; 2020s 197–8, 206, 221; 'Lionesses' identity 133

English Ladies' Football Association (ELFA) 67

Ennis-Hill, Jessica 130

equal pay: employer loopholes 46; Equal Pay Act (1970) 81; Equality Act (2010) 81n; footballers 6–7, 163–4, 199, 221; Nordic countries 6, 113; strike action 36, 46, 80–1; US 6, 47–8, 163–4, 199 *see also* employment equality

Ertz, Julie 135

European Competition for Women's Football (Euros precursor) 117

European Cup: 1957 (unofficial) 74; 1970s official plans 94

European Super League 213–15, 218, 223

Euros, Women's: 1989 precursor 117; 1991 108–9; 1995 110; 2005 148–9; 2017 143–6, 202; Germany's dominance 118; rising audience 146, 149, 202

Evening Standard (London) 30–2

Everard, Sarah 220

Everston, Ada 17

Everton 119, 169

factory workers: First World War 34–5, 36, 37–44; dismissals post First World War 46; Second World War 73; 1960s-1970s 80–1, 115; strike action 36, 46, 80–1 *see also* working-class women

fan movement and connection with players 218, 219–20

Farmer, Tony 184

Farr, Yvonne 96

fatality during men's football match 65

Faulkner, David 186

Fawcett Society 128, 129, 147

#FearlessFootball 162

Featherstone, Lynne 128

Felix, Allyson 131

femininity 14, 32, 66, 93, 94

feminists and feminism: contraception and sexual health 47, 79, 98; Lady Florence Dixie 22, 24, 25, 32; Nettie Honeyball 22–6; second wave 79, 98 *see also* suffrage and suffragettes; women's rights and equality

Ferris, Maggie 83, 84–5

FFIGC (Federazione Femminile Italiana Giuoco Calcio) 89

FICF (Federazione Italiana Calcio Femminile) 88–9

FIFA: attitudes to international competitions 89, 92, 94, 96–7; encourages women's teams 94; recognises first official match (1895) 21; suggests modified rules 94, 97 *see also* Women's World Cup

Filigno, Jonelle 132

financial crisis 2008, impact on women 128–9

financial support for women's football: during COVID-19 pandemic 207–11; FA distances itself from 86; France 124–6; future investment needs 224–5, 227–8, 230; by Premier League men's sides 8, 120, 121–2, 142, 169–70, 174, 176, 183, 188, 203, 224; role of international competitions 91, 127; US 100–2, 175, 223–4 *see also* professionalism; sponsorships

first official match recognised by FIFA (1895) 21

first recorded international match (1881) 4–5, 15–18

first Women's FA Cup final (1971) 85–6

First World War: women in the workforce 34–6; women's football resurgence 36–44

Fleeting, Julie 121

Follows, Sir Denis 82, 83–5

Football Association (FA): 1902 bans and restrictions 58; 1921 ban of women's football from FA-affiliated grounds 56–65; 1945 ban of women's football from all grounds in Scotland 74; 1962 confirms 1921 ban 82; 1970 lifts 1921 ban 82–6; 1972 keeps WFA at arm's length 86–7; 1992 takes over WFA 109–10; 2017 Gameplan for Growth and pyramid restructures 136–41, 145, 169–70, 173, 181–90; 2017 handling of racism scandal 152; 2017 switches from summer to winter league 169–70, 181–2, 202; 2019-21 handling of COVID-19 pandemic 206–13; board representation 217–18; finances 109–10; future as leader of women's football 222–3; marketing strategies 133–4; player contracts 178–9, 190,

211; societal influence 59–60 *see also* UEFA (Union of European Football Associations); Women's Championship; Women's FA Cup; Women's Football Association (WFA); Women's Premier League; Women's Super League

Footy Pups (children's TV show) 197

Fowler, Mary 166

France: 1932-1975 ban on women's football 66; hosts 2019 Women's World Cup 150, 154–64 *see also* France national team; *specific teams*

France Football Federation 123

France national team: 1960s-1970s 89, 92, 95, 96; 2010s 132, 143, 145, 155, 156, 157, 159

Frankfurt 119

Frankland, Alfred 41, 53, 64, 70, 71 *see also* Dick, Kerr Ladies

Franklin, Missy 131

Frauen-Bundesliga 117, 209

Fulham 197–8

fundraising *see* charity matches; financial support for women's football

future of women's football 221–30

Gameplan for Growth (FA) 136–41, 145, 169–70, 173

Germany: 1955-1970 DFB bans women's football in West Germany 66, 117; 1957 hosts unofficial European Cup 74; 1980s size of women's football in West Germany 91n; 1989 hosts European Competition for Women's Football 117; 2019-21 COVID-19 pandemic 209; Champions League dominance 119; Frauen-Bundesliga 117, 209;

national team 106, 108–9, 110, 112, 118–19, 134–5, 143; national team, East Germany 117; national team, West Germany 92, 117–18; Women's DFB Cup 118 *see also specific teams*
Glasgow Herald 15–16, 17
Glasgow Ladies 72
Glenn, Martin 135–6, 142
Goodwin, May 16
Gordon, Alec 17
Gore, Sylvia 108, 193
Göteborg 115
Gragt, Stefanie van der 144
Graham, George 120
Graham Hansen, Caroline 159
Graham, Mrs (Helen Matthews) 5, 32
Grainger, Katherine 130
The Graphic (magazine) 22
Gregory, Patricia 81–2, 84
Groenen, Jackie 163
Guardian (formerly *Manchester Guardian*) 20–1, 144, 152, 155, 171, 179, 227
Gunners (Arsenal) *see* Arsenal
Gustavsson, Tony 166

Hamm, Mia 193–4
Harder, Pernille 211
Harris, Jennie 191
Harrison, Abi 178
Hartlepool Northern Daily Mail 33
Haslam, Florrie 70
Havelange, Joáo 104
Hay, Ethel 16
Hayes, Emma 120, 228–9
Hayes United Ladies Football Club 71
healthcare provision 47, 48–9 *see also* maternity rights; medical welfare for players (lack of)
Heath, Tobin 135, 173, 211

Hegerberg, Ada 8, 16, 124, 143, 198–9, 225
Hegerberg, Andrine 16
Heinreichs, April 105
Hemsley, Julie 109
Hendricks, John 175
Hincks, Ashlee 178
history of women's football: ancient China, *cuju* ('kickball') 14–15; 18th century 14; 19th century 4–5, 6, 15–33, 57–8; early 20th century 33–4, 58; First World War 36–44; inter-War years 48–65, 67–71, 72, 88, 114, 191–2; Second World War 72, 73; post Second World War 74–5, 114; 1960s-1970s 74, 81–8, 89–97, 100–1, 103, 114–16, 117, 193; 1980s 91n, 103–5, 116, 117, 171; 1990s 105–12, 117–18, 121, 193–4, 195; 2000s 119, 121–7, 171, 175, 196; 2010s 102, 130–66, 169–74, 176–90, 197, 198, 199–203, 221; 2020s 102, 173, 174, 176, 178, 190, 199–200, 203–4, 206–17, 220–1
Hobbs, Arthur 81, 82, 85, 86–7
Hobbs, Nicola 7
Holiday, Lauren 135
Holloway, Norman 87
Holmes, Joseph 72
Honeyball, Nettie 22–6
Hong Kong, 1975 hosts Women's Asian Cup 103
Hopewell, Mabel, Maud and Minnie 16, 17
Horan, Lindsey 161
Houghton, Steph 158, 161, 169
Hull Daily Mail 32, 59–60
Hurst, Geoff 86
Hutson, Mary (Nettie Honeyball) 22–6

Independent 109, 110–11, 131
Infantino, Gianni 163

injuries to players: and 1921 FA ban 61–2; 1971 second unofficial Women's World Cup 95–6; poor treatment of injured players 174, 177–80

International Football Association Board 157

Ireland *see* Republic of Ireland; Team GB

Italian Cup 91

Italy: 1930s birth and death of women's football 88; 1961 hosts Corinthians and Nomads 74; 1968-1970 FICF and FFIGC founded 88–9; 1969-1980s hosts international competitions 89–90, 91, 92; 1970s European players drawn to 90–1; national team 89, 92, 96, 106; professionalism 88, 90–1 *see also specific teams*

Ivory Coast, national team 1, 104

Japan: 1981 hosts Mundialito 103; 2021 hosts 2020 Olympics 164–6; national team 104, 106, 111, 132, 134, 135, 158, 165

Jepson, Vicky 174

Johnson, Lyndon B. 99

Jones, Jade 131

Juventus 171, 215

Kaepernick, Colin 199, 200

Karim, Keramuddin 162

Kazakhstan, national team 147

Kell, Alice 52, 60–1, 70

Kennedy, John F. 99

Kenny, Laura 130

Kent, Major Cecil 63

Kerr, Sam 165–6

Khodayari, Sahar (#BlueGirl) 151

Kilmarnock Herald and North Ayrshire Gazette 53–4

Kirby, Fran 133, 158

Kirkland, Chris 174

kit *see* clothing and kit

Kmita, Rosie and Mollie 16

Knighton, Leslie 61

Kuvås, Målfrid 114–15

Lady Gaga 130

Lancashire Daily Post 62

Lancashire Evening Post 41–3, 56, 64–5

Latham, Kath 71–2

Lavelle, Rose 163, 211

Lazio 89, 90, 91

Leeds Mercury 57

Leicester 189

'Let Toys be Toys' campaign 25

Leuko, Yvonne 158

Lewes 189, 203

Lewis, John 43

LGBTQ+ rights 160, 199, 219

Li Guangyan (*cuju* player) 15

Liga Ellas (Spain) 176

Liga MX Femenil (Mexico) 202

Lincoln Ladies 169

Lindahl, Hedvig 163

Lindsey, Kelly 162

Liverpool 141, 169, 173–4, 215

Liverpool Echo 82–3

Ljungberg, Hanna 121

Lloyd, Carli 132, 135, 148

Lloyd George, David 45

Lockwood, Chris 95

Logan, Heidi 178

London Bees 178

Long, Miss A. (Strand Corner House Women's Football Team) 63–4

Lopez, Sue 81

Los Angeles Times 108

Lyon (Olympique Lyonnais) 122–7, 143, 198, 215

Lyons, Jan 90

male gaze: 19th century 20, 31–2;
post First World War 50; 1971
second unofficial Women's World
Cup 93 *see also* spectator attitudes
and behaviour
Malmö 115
Manchester City: infrastructure and
investment 122, 141, 170, 202–3;
wins place in WSL1 169, 188;
other mentions 178, 193, 204, 211
Manchester Corinthians 171, 193
Manchester Guardian see Guardian
(formerly *Manchester Guardian*)
Manchester United 142, 170–3, 187,
189, 204, 211, 215
Mannion, Aoife 178
Marin, Sanna 151
Markievicz, Constance 45–6
Marshall, Nellie 39
Marta (Marta Vieira da Silva) 121,
196–7
match reports: pre-19th century
accounts 13–14; 19th century 6,
15–16, 17, 18–21, 30–2; early 20th
century 33; First World War 37–9,
41–3; inter-War years 52–4, 56,
68–71; pre second World War 69–
70; international press 18, 68–9
maternity rights 6, 47, 221
Matthews, Helen (Mrs Graham)
5, 32
McWilliam, Peter 61
Mead, Beth 161
Medalen, Linda 105
media coverage *see* match reports;
*individual newspaper/magazine
titles*
medical welfare for players (lack of)
7, 170, 176–80, 211
Mellon, Kate 17
men vs women matches: early 20th
century 33; First World War 40;
post First World War 68–9, 114

#MeToo 147, 151, 200, 220
Mewis, Sam 211
Mexican Football Federation 92, 176
Mexico: 1971 hosts second unofficial
Women's World Cup 92–3,
95–6; Liga MX Femenil 202;
national team 92–3, 95, 132;
professionalism 176
middle- and upper-class women:
19th century attitudes towards
29–30; First World War voluntary
work 35–6; voting rights 45
Miedema, Vivianne 144, 145, 157, 166
Milano, Alyssa 147
Miliband, Ed 129
Milliat, Alice 55
mining communities, fundraising
for 53
Montpellier 123
Montreal Daily Mail 18
Moore, Leigh 133–4
Morgan, Alex 132, 161, 211
Morley, Joan 192
Mundialito (little World Cup) 89,
90, 103

Nagasato, Yūki 132, 135
National Joint Action Campaign
Committee for Women's Equal
Rights 80–1 *see also* women's
rights and equality
National Service Act (1941) 72–3
National Women's Soccer League
(NWSL) (US) 174–5, 176, 223–4
Naz, Jessica 178
Nchout, Ajara 158
Neid, Silvia 117–18
Nellis, Edna 90
Netherlands: 1959 hosts Corinthians
and Nomads 74; 2017 hosts
Euros 143–6; growth of women's
football 144; national team 104,
143–4, 145–6, 156–7, 162–3, 166

Neville, Phil 153–4, 160, 161–2, 165
Neville, Tracey 153
New York Sun 18
New York Times 93, 108
New Zealand, national team 106, 221
Newsham, Gail 40, 51–2, 58–9, 65, 71–2, 191–2
Newton, Katharine 152
Ngo Ndom, Annette 158
Nicholson, Raf 109
Nicollin, Louis 123
Nigeria, national team 106, 157, 221
Nixon, Richard 99
Nnadozie, Chiamaka 157
Nomads 74
Norfolk Chronical 33
Norris, Alice 59
Northern Ireland, Team GB 130–2, 165–6
Norway: Amazon Grimstad 114; BUL, Oslo 114–15; early women's football 114; first women's match 114; players' pay equality 6–7, 221; women's rights and equality 113–14 *see also* Hegerberg, Ada
Norway national team: 1980s 104, 105; 1990s 106, 111, 112, 116; 2010s 132, 143, 156, 159, 198; 2020s 221
Nottinghamshire Guardian 18–19
Notts County Ladies 182, 184
NWSL Challenge Cup (US) 211

O'Brien, Anne 90
Oceania Football Confederation (OFC) 104
OL Reign (formerly Reign FC) 126–7
Olympic Games: 1996 Atlanta 111–12; 2012 London 130–2; 2020 (held in 2021) Tokyo 164–6; Baron de Coubertin's warnings about women participants 131; Team GB 130–2, 165–6

Olympique Lyonnais (Lyon) 122–7, 143, 198, 215
Onguéné, Gabrielle 157
O'Reilly, Heather 148
Orlando Pride 197
Osaka, Naomi 199
Osborne, Bella 16
Öxabäcks 115, 116

Pankhurst, Christabel 46
Paris, Jasmin 151
Paris Saint-Germain 125, 143
Parliament (Qualification of Women) Act (1918) 45
Parr, Lily 52, 53–4, 69, 191–2
Parris, Nikita 155, 158, 160
Pathy, Jean-François 154–5
pay *see* equal pay
Pendleton, Vicky 130
period stigma and products 151, 220
Planned Parenthood 47
Poland, protests about banned abortion 220
police brutality and violence 30, 199, 200, 220
politicians, female 45–6
Politiken 178
Pomiès, Carmen 53
Popal, Khalida 162
Portugal, 1957 hosts Corinthians and Nomads 74
Premier League (men's): and COVID-19 match cancellations 209–10; financial support to women's football 8, 120, 121–2, 142, 169–70, 174, 176, 183, 188, 203, 224; influence on women's football 215, 217–18; possible takeover of WSL 222–3; Project Big Picture 213, 214, 215, 223; stadiums 110, 228 *see also* Women's Premier League
Press, Christen 160–1, 173, 211

press coverage *see* match reports; *individual newspaper titles*

Preston, Alfred 38, 39

Preston Ladies (formerly Dick, Kerr ladies) 39–44, 48, 51–6, 60–1, 64–5, 67–72, 191–2, 204

Priestman, Bev 166

professionalism: England 7, 120, 141–2, 169–70, 173–4, 177–90, 198, 208, 219–20; FIFA's global report into 176–7; Italy 88, 90–1; Spain 176; US 111, 174–6, 195, 223–4 *see also* financial support for women's football

Project Big Picture 213, 214, 215, 223

protests and activism: Black Lives Matter 220; #BlueGirl 151; civil rights 99, 147; climate change 151; corruption in Sudan 151; early years childcare provision 130; equal pay 80, 163–4; #FearlessFootball 162; by footballers/athletes 1–2, 6–7, 159–60, 163–4, 198–200, 219, 221; LGBTQ+ rights 160, 199, 219; #MeToo 147, 151, 200, 220; period stigma and products 151, 220; police brutality 199, 200, 220; sexual health and abortion 47, 130, 220; 'Slut Walk' 129–30; suffrage 47; taking the knee 1–2, 199, 200 *see also* strike action

Punch (magazine) 13

Qatar, national team 131

racism scandal in English team 152

Rafferty, Claire 134, 179–80

Rafferty, Laura 178

Raisman, Aly 131

Rance, Miss (Dick, Kerr Ladies) 43

Rapinoe, Megan 132, 159–60, 163–4, 199–200, 225–7

Rashford, Marcus 2

Raw, Louise 27

Rayman, Rose 17

Reading Evening Post 111

Real Madrid 171, 215

Redfearn, Neil 173–4

Redford, Florrie 53, 191

Reign FC 126–7

Reilly, Rose 90

Reims 90

Renard, Wendie 156, 157

Renzulli, Peter 69

Representation of the People Act (1918) 45

Republic of Ireland: pay dispute 6–7, 221; rugby 205

Riise, Hege 165

Riweford, Maud 17

Robinson, J. W. 38

Roma 89, 90

Rous, Sir Stanley 96–7

rules: 1921 *Barnet Press* satirical article 49–51; 1970s FIFA suggests modifications 94, 97; 1988-1991 eighty minute cap on early Women's World Cup matches 105; 1995 two-minute timeouts in each half 108; 2019/2020 Laws of the Games 157–8; pitch and goal sizes 228–9

Russia, 1917 strike action 36

Rutherglen Ladies 72

Sakaguchi, Mizuho 132

Sampson, Mark 146, 152

Sanderson, Lianne 152

Sanger, Margaret 47

Sanguinetti, Michael 129–30

Saudi Arabia, national team 131

#SayHerName 220

Scharlieb, Mary 61–2

Scholes, Charles 17

school PE and football (UK) 3–4, 138–41, 212

Scotland: vs England, 19th century matches 4–5, 15–21; national team 90, 108, 155, 193; pay and conditions dispute 6–7, 221; Scottish FA 74, 90, 221; Team GB 130–2, 165–6

Scott, Alex 7, 121, 133

Scott, Jill 159, 169

Scudetto 90, 91

Second World War 72–3, 79

Sex Disqualification (Removal) Act 1919 46

Sha, Zukang 128

SheBelieves Cup 143, 161, 206

Sheffield Daily Telegraph 38–9, 57

Sheffield United 189

Sherwood, Nelly 17

Sibbet, Grace 40

Sidney, Sir Philip 13

Sierra Leone, national team 221

Simmons, Kelly 109–10, 138–9, 142, 181–2, 187

Sinclair, Christine 132

sisters, football-playing 16, 17

The Sketch (magazine) 22–6

'Slut Walk' protests 129–30

Smith, C. and S. 38, 39

Smith, Kelly 121, 142, 195–6

Smith, Phoebe 22

social media communication strategies 133

Sonja Henie 114

South America, 1960 hosts Corinthians and Nomads 74

South American Football Confederation (CONMEBOL) 104

South Korea, national team 155

Southampton 85, 87, 90, 189

Spain: 1935-1980 ban on women's football 66; professionalism and Liga Ellas 176

spectator attitudes and behaviour: 19th century 5, 19–21; First World War 42–3; post First World War 51–2; 1980s 118; 2019 Women's World Cup 157 *see also* male gaze

spectator numbers *see* attendance at matches (recent years)

Spence, Drew 152

sponsorships: 1970s 91, 92, 94; 1990s 105, 111; 2010s 154–5, 163, 164, 175; 2020s 174, 215–16, 217, 223–4; individual players 194, 198

Sporting Life 58

St Clair, Lily 16, 17

stadiums, and attendance 202–5, 228

Stanley, Alice 55

Star Green 'Un (Sheffield) 58

Starling, Maud 17

Stevenson, Isa 16, 17

Stewarton and Thistle 85

Stoke Ladies 67

Stoney, Casey 173

Strand Corner House Women's Football Team 63

strike action: students 129; workers 36, 46, 80–1 *see also* protests and activism

suffrage and suffragettes: Lady Florence Dixie 22, 24, 25, 32; Nordic countries 113; Representation of the People Act (1918) 45; US 47; violence towards suffragettes 30 *see also* feminists and feminism; women's rights and equality

Sunderland 182, 183, 185, 188

Sundhage, Pia 91

supporter ownership model 203

Sweden: 1995 hosts second official Women's World Cup 108, 110–11; Champions League dominance 119; early women's football 114; growth of women's football 115–16, 144; national team 104,

105, 106, 111, 112, 116, 162–3, 166; women's rights and equality 113–14 *see also specific teams*
Swedish Cup 196
Swedish Football Federation 115–16
Switzerland, national team 117
Sydney Evening News 18

taking the knee 1–2, 199, 200
Taylor, Breonna 220
Taylor, Jodie 145, 156
Taylor, Louise 144
Team GB 130–2, 165–6
Telegraph 84
Thailand, national team 104
'This Girl Can' campaign 14
Thunberg, Greta 151
Title IX of the Education Amendments (US) 99–102, 103, 106
Torrent, Marion 156
Tottenham 178, 204, 211
Tower, John 100
Trott, Laura 130
Trump, Donald 159–60
Turbine Potsdam 119

UEFA (Union of European Football Associations): 1950s no women's competitions 74; 1969-1970 puts pressure on FA 82; 1971 establishes committee for women's football 93–4; 1980s European tournaments 108; 1988 representation at Women's World Cup feasibility tournament 104 *see also* Champions League, women's (formerly UEFA Women's Cup); Euros, Women's
Umeå IK 119, 121, 196
United States national team (USWNT): 1980s 89–90, 104, 105; 1990s 106–8, 193–4; 2010s

131, 132, 134, 135, 159–62, 163–4, 221; 2020s 166, 199–200, 211, 221; other mentions 91, 102, 198
United States of America: 1909 strike action 36; 1972 Title IX of the Education Amendments 99–102, 103, 106; First World War 35; Civil Rights Act (1964) 99; college sport 100–1, 194; early women's football 68; Equal Rights Amendment 47–8; hosts 1996 Olympics 111–12; hosts Dick, Kerr Ladies 67–9; maternity and childcare 47; national team *see* United States national team (USWNT); OL Reign (formerly Reign FC) 126–7; pay and conditions dispute 221; professionalism 111, 174–6, 195, 223–4; SheBelieves Cup 143, 161, 206; suffrage 47; winning mentality 161–2; Women's Joint Congressional Committee 47; working women 35, 47–8
United States Soccer Federation 175
USA Today 108

Vance, Mabel 17
VAR (Video Assistant Referee) 156, 157–8
Vasco de Gama 196
Vasstøl, Else 114
Veenendaal, Sari van 163
Vintner, Geraldine 17

Wales, Team GB 130–2, 165–6
Walker, Miss (Dick, Kerr Ladies) 52
Wall, Frederick 62–3
Wambach, Abby 132
Ward, Carla 174
Washington Herald 68
Washington Post 68–9
Wembley Ladies 195

Wenger, Arsène 121
West Ham 170, 189, 204
Western Morning News 70–1
White, Ellen 155, 158, 160, 161, 165, 166
White, Faye 121
White Ribbon 81–2
Whitehead, Linda 109
Whittle, Miss (Dick, Kerr, Ladies) 43
Whitworth, Margaret 90
Wiegman, Sarina 165
Wille, Ellen 103–4
Williams, Fara 7, 133
Williams, Jean 68
Williams, Serena 131, 199
Wilson, Carole 96
Wilson, Harold 79–80
Wolfsburg 119
women vs men matches: early 20th century 33; First World War 40; post First World War 114; 1920s (US tour of Dick, Kerr Ladies) 68–9
Women's Asian Cup 103
women's Champions League 119, 121, 122, 124, 196, 198, 210
Women's Championship 170, 182, 186, 189–90, 203, 211, 214, 223
Women's Cricket World Cup 146
Women's DFB Cup 118
Women's Euros *see* Euros, Women's
Women's FA Cup 142, 202, 214
women's football *see* future of women's football; history of women's football; *specific countries; specific governing bodies; specific players; specific teams*
Women's Football Association (WFA): 1969 founding 81; 1971 criticises second unofficial Women's World Cup 96; 1971 establishes England team 108; 1972 kept at arm's length by

FA 86–7; 1992 takeover by FA 109–10; financial support 86, 87; Scottish Women's FA 90
Women's Joint Congressional Committee (US) 47
Women's Premier League 110, 121, 183
Women's Professional Soccer league (US) 175
women's rights and equality: abortion 80, 130, 220; employment equality 113, 128; equal pay *see* equal pay; National Joint Action Campaign Committee for Women's Equal Rights 80–1; role of football in promoting (in general) 2–3, 137, 200, 225, 226–7, 228–30; standing for election to Parliament 45; Title IX of the Education Amendments (US) 99–102, 103, 106; voting *see* suffrage and suffragettes; working in the armed forces 72–3; working in the civil or judicial service 46 *see also* feminists and feminism; protests and activism
Women's Super League (WSL): broadcast rights 216; and COVID-19 pandemic 208–10, 211; future of 222–3, 224; launch 169; and Project Big Picture 214; restructures 142, 169–70, 181–90; stadiums and attendance 201, 202–4; WSL2 169, 170; other mentions 119, 217–18 *see also* Women's Championship
Women's United Soccer Association (US) 175
Women's World Cup: 1988 feasibility tournament 104–5; 1991 first official tournament 105–6, 193; 1995 second official tournament

108, 110–12, 118; 1999 193; 2003 and 2007 118, 196; 2015 132–5, 150; 2019 147–8, 150, 154–64, 197, 200; inadequate FIFA investment 225–6; prize money 150, 230; rising audience 164; unofficial tournaments 89, 92–3, 94–6 *see also* FIFA

Woods, Miss (Dick, Kerr Ladies) 52

workers' rights *see* equal pay

working-class women: 19th century attitudes towards 27–9; First World War roles 34–6; post First World War dismissals 46; strike action 36, 46, 80–1; voting rights 45 *see also* factory workers

World Cup *see* Women's World Cup

World Wars *see* First World War; Second World War

Wright, Emma 16, 17

Wright, Georgina 16

Yankey, Rachel 121, 197–8

Yates, 'Glaxo' (Preston Ladies) 70

Yeovil 183–4

Yorkshire Post and Leeds Intelligencer 65

Zambia, national team 166